PRINCES, POTENTATES, AND PLAIN PEOPLE

PRINCES, POTENTATES, AND PLAIN PEOPLE

The Saga of the Germans from Russia

by
REUBEN GOERTZ

The Center for Western Studies

The Prairie Plains Series Number 3

Published by
The Center for Western Studies
Box 727, Augustana College
Sioux Falls, South Dakota 57197

The Center for Western Studies is an archives, library, museum, publishing house and educational agency concerned principally with collecting, preserving, and interpreting prehistoric, historic, and contemporary materials that document native and immigrant cultures of the northern prairie plains. The Center promotes understanding of the region through exhibits, publications, art shows, conferences, and academic programs. It is committed, ultimately, to defining the contribution of the region to American civilization.

The Prairie Plains Series is dedicated to the publication at moderate prices of essential but limited-market titles.

Printed by Pine Hill Press, Inc., Freeman, South Dakota.

Library of Congress Cataloging-in-Publication Data:

Goertz, Reuben, 1918-1993.
        Princes, potentates, and plain people : the saga of the Germans from Russia / by Reuben Goertz.
        p. cm. —(The prairie plains series : no. 3)
        Includes bibliographical references.
        ISBN 0-931170-59-1 (cloth) : $23.95. — ISBN 0-931170-58-3 (paper) : $13.95
        1. Russian Germans—South Dakota—History. 2. Russian Germans—South Dakota—Social life and customs. 3. South Dakota—History. 4. South Dakota—Social life and customs. I. Title. II. Series.
F660.R85P75 1994
978.3'0049171043—dc 20
                                      94-40155
                                        CIP

Jacket/Cover illustration:
        Unlike the sod huts and dugouts of their neighbors, the houses of the Germans from Russia were built to last. Typical of their sturdy dwellings is the rock-and-brick homestead where Florence Gering Goertz was born and raised. It was built north of Yankton, Dakota Territory, in 1875 by her grandfather John Gering and styled after those in Volhynia Poland, where he had been born in 1847. With his wife Maria Graber, Gering came to America in 1874 with three small daughters; one died on the way to the settlement. Seven more children and four granddaughters were born in the house, which was dismantled in 1946.

P27
33
53
60
109-110
111
115
136-137
153
178

Table of Contents

POLISH WOLHYNIEN = WESTERN VOLHYNIA.
TO POLAND 1920± – 1940±
 UKRAINE 1992± —
 USSR - 1940± – 1992±
 ROVNO = CAPITAL ±

1918-1993

A Tribute

This is but a kaleidoscope of a man who lived life to the full. He read, he studied, he wrote with delight, vigor and contentment. He was an inspired word painter, with a flowing beauty in his lyrics that has an appeal like that of beautiful music. He wrote with great fascination of

> Literary history
> Philosophical expressiveness
> Psalm-like probing and a
> Great appreciation of past events.

Life was a rich experience, every moment precious, every sensation a treasure.
His life was an inspiration.
His memory a benediction.

—Florence Goertz

Preface

I was deeply moved, and at the same time honored, when Mrs. Florence (Jimmy) Goertz and her family asked me to write the preface to this fine collection of papers written by their beloved husband and father, and my special friend and colleague, Reuben Goertz.

These papers were presented at a wide variety of conferences, meetings, and professional organizations over a period of many years. They were selected by his wife and family, in consultation with the staff of the Center for Western Studies, from the very large collection of his papers now deposited in the archives of the Center, as was his wish.

Reuben possessed an exceptional gift for writing, coupled with a special talent and flair for speaking, that is readily apparent in these papers.

I have been associated, by virtue of my professional career, with a wide variety of people, professional and lay persons, and can honestly state that Reuben Goertz ranked among the highest in so many qualities. Others may have better formal educations, advanced degrees, and professional experience, but he spent his lifetime in intensive study, research, and travel pursuing his lifelong interest, the history and culture of his people, the Germans from Russia. He took pride in the fact that he was largely self-educated, but he became one of the nation's experts on this culture and tradition. He was so knowledgeable that he was continually called upon for information, or to present papers on his specialty.

However, in my opinion and based on a close relationship with him over many years, the qualities that separated him from most others were his insatiable desire for honesty, dignity, integrity, and unselfishness in all his relationships with family, friends and colleagues. He was a humble, sensitive, self-effacing man. Often I heard him say in all seriousness,

"I'm no more than a poor rural mail carrier. I can't compete with all you Ph.D.'s!"

Mutual trust was his watchword. He firmly believed in verbal agreements and detested the fact that legal douments had to be prepared in order to assure that one's wishes would be carried out. I well remember how difficult it was for him to sign the papers, that I attempted to explain were necessary, at the time he decided to deposit his collection at the Center for Western Studies. He continually stated, "You're an honest man . . . I'm an honest man . . . our word is our bond . . . we do not need to sign papers to insure that what we want is the way it will be." He chided me about this for many years.

Conversations with Reuben were always "happenings." He told stories with a flair that combined historical information and fact with a humor and sensitivity that few could match. He could spellbind a group at any level in a delightful manner.

His collection of papers will remind all who knew and admired him that we have lost not only a dear friend, but a living encyclopedia of knowledge about his people, the Germans from Russia.

By all who knew Reuben these papers will be read as if he were speaking, and these people will be reminded of his stories and his special gift for illustrating his remarks.

To others, something may be lost in the written form that was so very meaningful in the oral presentation. For this we do not apologize . . . we can only state that "something is missing, and that something is Reuben," a sad fact that we cannot change. However, the content and significance of each paper is apparent.

—Dr. Sven G. Froiland
Emeritus Director
The Center for Western Studies

Introduction

Reuben Goertz and I met for the first time at a convention of the American Historical Society of German from Russia (AHSGR) at Boulder, Colorado, on 7-11 June 1972. Both of us had been invited to speak at this convention. I presented a paper on "The Migrations of Germans from Russia to the Americas"; he gave a slide lecture on "German Russian Homes" built by immigrant pioneers in South Dakota. His lecture, with some added information obtained on subsequent trips to Europe, was published in the 1976 edition of the AHSGR periodical *Clues.* It is this 1976 version that appears in the present book.

Because our interests were so much alike, both of us very interested in the history of our German-Russian forefathers, Reuben and I spent much time together at this convention. We met again at another AHSGR convention in Fresno, California, in June 1974. On that occasion I introduced to the convention-eers my book, *From Catherine to Khrushchev, The Story of Russia's Germans,* which had just come off the press, and he presented "Wedding Bells Ringing," a humorous description of marriage customs among his German-Russian forefathers in South Dakota, which appears among his papers published here.

Our meetings at conventions occurred annually over the years, and in between we often corresponded on matters of interest. After I became president of AHSGR in 1978 and then, in 1981, editor of the *Journal,* I often had to visit AHSGR headquarters in Lincoln, Nebraska. On such trips, a visit in Freeman, South Dakota, with Reuben and Florence (Jimmy), when time permitted, was an added pleasure. I saw the Goertz Collection, as it was then, and, because I was accumulating a similar collection, I examined some of the items with great interest. Our conversations on such occasions often went on far into the night.

The sources of Reuben's lectures and writings presented in this book were mainly three: (1) stories told by his grandmother and other relatives and friends of the older generation in South Dakota; (2) written materials about the history of his forefathers that he gathered over the years, the Goertz Collection; and (3) trips to the European regions in which his forefathers and their co-religionists had lived.

The stories he heard from his elders, with which he entertained many gatherings over the years, gave him an abiding interest in the history of his Mennonite forefathers in the old world. It became imperative for him to see the places where they had lived and where some his people still live. With his equally interested wife accompanying him, he went on tours of Europe two summers in succession, 1972 and 1973. On the first tour they visited areas of Poland and the Ukraine, in which there had been thriving Mennonite settlements, now inhabited by others. In 1973 they visited various parts of western Europe: the Zurich region in Switzerland, in which the Swiss Mennonites (among them Reuben's forebears) originated; the region of Montbeliard in eastern France, where Swiss Mennonites had settled before the area had become French; and Weierhof in the Palatinate, where an old Mennonite community is still thriving. Following these tours, Reuben wrote interesting descriptions of his experiences, which are reproduced in this book.

"Odyssey" is a rambling account of the story of the Germans from Russia, with special attention to the Mennonites. It mentions their home areas in Germany, why they migrated to Russia, their settlements in Russia, why some of them left these to come to America, their settlements in South Dakota and elsewhere in the United States, and their gradual assimilation. Included is a description of some of the places in the Ukraine that Reuben's group visited during their 1972 tour.

"The Mountains Are My Sanctuary" is am ambitious venture into a very complex period of European history, the

Reformation. The revolt against Middle Ages Catholicism by
Luther and Zwingli in the 1520s, which developed into Lutheran and Reformed churches, also had offshoots led by less
well-known reformers: Blaurock, Felix Manz, Conrad Grebel,
Jacob Hutter, and others, in Switzerland, who promoted
Anabaptist views. Because Reuben's forefathers were followers
of this minority Reformation tendency, he gave special study to
it. In this article, he traces his group of Swiss Anabaptists
through the persecutions of their early years, to a safe haven
eventually, for a time, in Moravia, where they became community Hutterites, then to Transylvania in Hungary, from there
to the Ukraine, and finally to America. Because of my own
limited knowledge of the complexities of Reformation history,
I find parts of this story difficult to follow.

"Princes, Potentates, and Plain People" deals with the
contacts of plain people (Mennonites) with members of the
ruling classes: a wealthy Polish aristocrat, a Duke of Württem-
berg, Marie Theresa and Joseph II of Austria, Frederick the
Great of Prussia, Catherine II, Paul I, and Alexander I of
Russia, and finally President Grant of the United States. A
section of this article of special interest to us deals with the
visit of Reuben's tour group in 1973 to the French-speaking
Swiss Mennonites in Montbeliard in eastern France.

Although the three historical writings described above are
good reading, they are not Reuben at his best. He was more
relaxed and more at home with stories of events that occurred
among his own people in South Dakota. These gave him more
scope for his characteristic sense of humor, which sparkled in
his conversation and in his speeches. He was a master storyteller. Two of his presentations printed in this book, "Wedding
Bells Ringing," mentioned earlier, and "Ye Olde Morality,"
which deal humorously with the marriage customs among the
Mennonite pioneers in South Dakota, and his description in
"My Sullied Saints" of many other humorous events in the life
of his people, are good illustrations of his style. Even when he

is dealing with sadder events, as in "Pioneering in Dakota Territory," there are many flashes of humor. His skill as a storyteller is illustrated particularly well also in the following: his comparison of Volga German customs with those of Mennonites in "An Irreverent Mennonite Casts Sidelong Glances at his Volga Compatriots"; his description of an anti-German episode in 1921 in South Dakota in "Reinhold DeWald and Relief Cattle for Germany"; and his story of a Mennonite missionary in China, who died abroad and came home as a mummy, in "From Missionary to Mummy." He also did some interesting research on folktales that he heard from his elders, and discovered, as he explained in "Folktales—Facts or Fiction," that some of them were based on actual events in the history of his forefathers.

There is an interesting account of the religious history of the Mennonites in South Dakota in "Chapel Talk." This deals especially with the changes in the religious attitudes among these Mennonites over a century, during which three different groups of them accommodated to intermarriage with each other and eventually to intermarriage with non-Mennonite neighbors. Difficult in the early years, this became easier as people who differed in religion learned to know each other. It is obvious that Reuben considered the change a healthy development.

In his later years, he tended to become philosophical in his speeches. This tendency appears to some extent in several of his presentations mentioned above, but the best description of this philosophy of life is in "What's the Use?" This is, in my opinion, the *best of his speeches* published in this book. He was speaking to a fiftieth anniversary reunion of the class of 1938 at Freeman Junior College. He reviewed life as he and his classmates had seen it, with its many ups and down in those fifty years. He found examples of healthy attitudes in difficult times in King Solomon and, in more detail, in the life of Abraham Lincoln. He ended with a well-chosen quotation, found on a scrap of paper in Old Saint Paul's Church in Baltimore in 1692.

We can be confident that, when Reuben entered the pearly gates, the angels welcomed him with smiles!

—Dr. Adam Giesinger
University of Manitoba
Winnipeg, Manitoba

German Russian Homes: Here and There, Now and Then

Given at the June 1972 convention of the American Historical Society of Germans from Russia at Boulder, Colorado.

The simple but sturdy old earthen homes that still sparsely dot the landscape around my home town of Freeman, South Dakota, are the most obvious, tangible link with my grandparents, who helped build similar homes a century ago. Built during a short period of five years, these homes dominated the unbroken grassland vista wherever the German settlers from Russia put down their claim stakes. The dugout in the side of a creek bank or the sod shanty hastily thrown together as a temporary shelter are not germane to this discussion since we are concerned with the first permanent homes erected here.

In 1873 the railroad came to Yankton, Dakota Territory. This facilitated the homesteading process. In 1874, what had been a trickle of settlers became a flood as immigrants poured from the train in Yankton. The Germans from Russia filled Hutchinson County, at that time a two-day journey from Yankton, and overflowed into neighboring Turner and McCook Counties. The desperate housing situation for these newcomers was aggravated by the long distance from the source of supply of building materials. This wasn't the overriding factor. The lack of money put these materials as far out of reach as did the distance. So for five years these ingenious people built substantial homes out of those materials readily at hand: dirt, rock and grass. In 1879 the Chicago, Milwaukee, Saint Paul and Pacific Railroad extended its line from Marion Junction to Running

Water on the Missouri River, and towns like Freeman and
Menno sprang up along the right of way in the midst of these
German settlers. Heretofore scarce building materials became
readily available, and by helping build the railroad the pioneers
earned their first hard cash with which to buy these commo-
dites. Now, after only five years the homes of dirt, rock and
grass gave way to the frame houses built of wood.

As I first looked at these old homes, I marveled at the
resourcefulness of these old-timers. I delighted in their
inventiveness and adaptability. Then, slowly, came the
dawning of a vague suspicion that maybe they hadn't improvised. Maybe they had just transplanted home styles to the
prairies as they had transplanted their strange life styles and
foreign language. When an unexpected opportunity presented
itself to visit those places in Russia where my grandparents
had been born, my wife and I arranged to go to see. We received
an unanticipated assist in our search in the person of the
intourist guide assigned to our group. Our guide shared our
interest in old buildings. Her name was Nina.

While Nina was guiding us through one of the older
classical buildings in Kiev, she said in faultless English and
with obvious pride, "It is as our great writer Nikolai Gogol has
written, 'Architecture is the chronicle of the world. It speaks to
us long after legends die, long after songs and poems become
silent'."

At that a happy little voice in my heart cheerfully
chortled, "Yes! Yes! Yes!" But in my head another voice, a
nagging voice, incessantly raised the question, "But Nina, have
your people left anything of the architecture of my people so
that it may speak to me while their legends still live? While
their songs and poems still flow from countless lips?" I was
reluctant to give voice to the question because of a foreboding
fear that everything her ancestors and mine had built had long
since been destroyed by a violent revolution, a world war, and
hostile natives.

To show what my wife and I were looking for in Russia, this article will include old photographs and new pictures of some of the old homes in the Freeman, South Dakota, area. There are pictures of similar homes in Russia photographed in 1971 and 1973. Not only will we be spanning an ocean and two continents in distance but a century in time. For written comment I will quote primarily from Noble Prentis who wrote about these "strange" new people and their unique homes during their early years in Kansas for the readers of the *Topeka Commonwealth*. Why quote a Kansas writer to describe South Dakota homes? There are several reasons.

First, these were not only South Dakota houses: they were of a universal style used by the Germans from Russia wherever they settled from Kansas to Canada.

Secondly, there were no Hutterite colonies in Kansas to confuse the writer. To this day writers and historians in South Dakota seemingly cannot differentiate between the colony Hutterite, who wears garments of basic black and stays closely confined to his colony, and a Mennonite like myself, who wears anything he can lay his hands on and wanders all over the state trying for all the world to look like a Methodist.

Finally, I like the Prentis style. Inflexibly honest and brutually frank, he praised the praiseworthy and varnished the ugly parts with humor. His brief description of the men who built these homes could be about any of my grandparents' peer group:

"The men seem to have conscientious scruples against wearing clothes that fit them," wrote Prentis, "the idea appearing to be to get all the cloth you can for the money. Their vests therefore descend toward their knees and their pants possess an alarming amount of slack. Their favorite head gear appears to be a flat black cloth cap which they pull off in saluting anyone they meet—a habit they will soon forget now that they have arrived in Kansas were nobody respects nothing."

The Mendel House near Freeman, South Dakota an example of the house-barn combination built with native materials, with straw roof and containing a Russian oven.

The Mendel House on the banks of the James River west of Freeman incorporated the four basic criteria of those early homes that I was going to look for in Russia:

1. *The House Barn Combination.* Those of us who have read Rolvaag's *Giants in the Earth* could easily be led to believe that the idea of a house and barn built as a single unit was conceived by Rolvaag's hero, Per Hansa, in eastern South Dakota several years before the arrival of our ancestors. I could not abide the thought of a fictitious Norwegian striding across the pages of Rolvaag's novel and getting credit for something I instinctively knew our people had been doing longer and better. I had to find a house-barn combination predating the arrival of Rolvaag on the American scene.

2. *The Straw Roof.* This building, like all the other original buildings of this genre, had a straw roof. Mr. Mendel wrote how the heavy snows during the winter of 1880-81 caused many straw roofs to collapse. In this particular home the debris from the fallen roof blocked the doors, and the livestock in the barn had to be hoisted over the walls to be removed from the shambles. I hoped to see a straw roof in Russia. I had never seen a straw roof. I couldn't even imagine one. Every time I tried to visualize a straw roof on this building, the first of the three little pigs would intrude on my fantasy, the one that built the house of straw and had it blown in by the Big Bad Wolf—a Russian wolf no doubt.

3. *A Russian Oven.* The thing that most impressed non-German neighbors and visiting journalists about these homes was the *Russian oven.* The efficient grass burner was a sensation. As coal became available, these immense brick ovens were replaced with new metal stoves. Mr. Mendel left a written account of the Russian oven in this house and its metal successor. Even if the Russians don't have Russian salad dressing, they would surely have a Russian oven.

4. *The Use of Native Materials.* The use of grass in these buildings was not confined to the thatched roof. Grass, and especially flax straw when it became available, was mixed into the mud. The type of dirt used was not too important to the builder, and the same building will reveal that clay and black top soil were used indiscriminately. The dirt and grass were mixed by having horses or oxen walk back and forth over the mixture as water was added. One pioneer recalls that in one instance sheep were used. In Russia, after the bolsheviks had confiscated all the live stock, the women did the mixing with their bare feet. The mortar was mixed to such a consistency that it could be handled with a pitch fork. Some builders forked the mud into a form. In most instances there was no lumber for a form and the walls were shaped with a short board held in each hand of the construction foreman. Without the use of a form the walls could not be built higher than two or three feet

in one day lest the weight of the material would cause the walls to spread. In a few instances the mortar was made into bricks which were sun dried and then laid into walls. To protect the outside walls from the elements, they were stuccoed with lime made from local limestone.

Since cracks in the stucco had to be filled annually, one Abraham Weins elected to nail shiplap to the outside walls. Homes like this one moved Noble Prentis to write, "The people are like their houses, useful but ugly." Evidently the practical advantages of these homes far outweighed any esthetic consideration, and he wrote glowingly of the *Russian oven*. One still exists in this house.

Wrote Prentis, "An immense pile of straw was intended, Mr. Wiebe said, for fuel this winter. The Mennonites are economists in the way of fuel, and at the houses are large piles of chopped straw mixed with barnyard manure stacked up for 'firewood.' This kind of fuel destroys one's ideas of the 'cheerful fireside' and 'blazing hearth.' There is not much 'Yulelog' poetry about it. Straw sounds and smells better. In order to use it, however, the Mennonites discard stoves and use a *Russian oven* built in the wall of the house, which, once thoroughly heated with light straw, will retain its warmth longer than young love itself."

Another time he advised his readers, "He exhibited his *Russian oven,* built in the partition walls so as to warm two or three rooms, and to which is attached also a sort of brick range for cooking purposes. This device cannot be explained without a diagram. It is perfectly efficient, and the smoke at last goes into a wide chimney which is used as the family smoke house."

In Nebraska, J. D. Butler echoed the sentiments of Prentis in Kansas. "Aware that such generalities are too vague, I will make my description more specific, and since the eye catches in an instant what the ear cannot learn in an hour, I have also had a diagram prepared which will render the whole mystery plain and level to the lowest capacity."

"The grass furnace or stove is nothing costly, or complicated, or likely to get out of order. On the other hand it is a contrivance so simple that many will say of it as one man did when he first saw a railroad track: 'Nobody but a fool could have thought of so simple a thing!' In a word, as the Irishman made a cannon by taking a large hole and pouring iron around it, so the Mennonite mother of food and warmth is developed by piling brick or stones around the hollow.

"Straw and old prairie grass have been thought as useless as grave stones after the resurrection. But the recent utilizing of them is in keeping with the spirit of age . . ." ("The Mennonite Stove," pamphlet, 1877, reprinted in *Mennonite Life* 4.4 [October 1949]: 16-17).

Both Butler and Prentis erred in assuming that the *grass burner* was strictly a Mennonite device. They were widely used by non-Mennonite Germans from Russia all over Hutchinson County. In Russia I asked Nina if she could show me a *Russian oven.* She looked at me blankly. Like Prentis and Butler, I sketched a diagram and her face lit up with happy recognition. "Oh! But of course! You mean a German oven!" she exclaimed.

UKRAINIAN OVEN

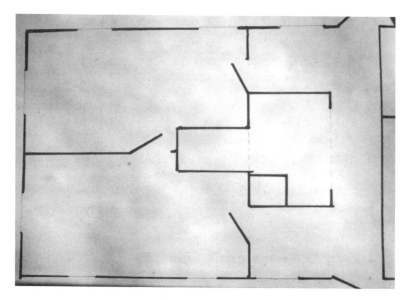

Russian oven at center; cooking range, left center; double sliding doors into oven at right.

She then explained how I would be able to differentiate between homes built by Ukrainians and Germans. Homes built by Ukrainians usually had three windows in the gable end of the house. Since the Germans extended the range part of the oven to the next wall, it usurped that place the Ukrainians used for the middle window. Most German homes had only two windows in the gable end.

The first fire of the day was often kindled by materials readily available on the other side of the door that opened into the barn part of the building, the straw and hay stems not consumed by the livestock during the night. Again quoting J. D. Butler: "How is the grass prepared or pressed for the fire-box? It is not prepared at all, but is thrust in with a fork as one would throw fodder into a rack. People suppose they must be putting in this fuel all the time. This is not fact. At the house of Bishop Peters (48 x 27 feet), which is a large one for a new country, the grass or straw is pitched in for about twenty minutes twice, or at most three times, in twenty-four hours. That amount of firing up suffices both for cooking and comfort." The attributes of grass as a fuel were explained in an article in *Zur Heimath* by C. L. Bernays (1878; reprinted in *Mennonite Life* 4.4 [October 1949]: 20): "Because of the lack of firewood, straw is used for fuel; but in the first year, when the new settlers had no straw, they mowed grass and heated the stoves with dried hay. They were, therefore, called 'grass-burners.' Now only straw is used for heating everywhere. Once or twice a day heavy straw bundles are stuffed into the stove with a pitchfork, then the straw is lit. It smoulders slowly and requires much less attention than a wood fire."

This ornate brick structure is a chimney of a *Russian oven* on the Elmer Grosz farm in the Wittenberg area of Hutchinson County. Note the door on the right of the chimney for inserting and removing meats and sausage for smoking. When the meats were smoked they were buried in the piles of oats stored in the attics of these homes.

After the oven was thoroughly warmed, the ashes were scraped out. To remove the last vestige of ashes before the dough was inserted for baking, the *Haus Frau* would toss a handful of flour into the oven. The resultant explosion would expell the most obstinate ash particles with a sudden "Woosh!"

Homes like the frame house built by Ludwig Deckert in the Freeman area prompted Noble Prentis to comment, "A few of the wealthier citizens had built frame houses, furnished with the brick ovens of Russian origin which warm the family and cook its food for all day with two armfuls of loose straw."

The grandchildren recall that Grandpa Deckert would tell how on a hot day the oxen would walk into any available body of water with their loads of lumber on the long trek back from Yankton. This would be a good indication that this house too was built before the advent of the railroad in 1879.

When my wife and I travelled to Russia and Poland my questions about the architecture of my people began to be

The John H. Waltner home built by Ludwig Deckert, also in the Freeman area, was a sign of affluence.

answered. Our Polish guides showed us something our Russian guides couldn't or wouldn't. We were shown an abundance of straw or thatched roofs.

In Russia, however, we were able to see from our bus window straw roofs on contemporary homes. We also began to

Since wood was abundant in the Volhynian province, formerly Russian but now in Poland, the homes were built of wood and not of earth.

POLAHD,
1920 ±
1940±

/992 ± = UKRAINE

see the other features I was looking for—the use of native materials, the house-barn combination, and evidence of the *Russian oven.*

The eight photographs that follow illustrate many of the similarities between the homes in the Freeman, South Dakota, area and those seen in Poland and Russia: a photo from near Dubno and Lvov shows the characteristic earthen walls and straw roof. The Gering house is of home-made brick; the Hofer house once contained a Russian oven. A house in western Russia reveals the house-barn style. The Lang, Kleinsasser, and Zanter houses illustrate the ingenious use of earth as a building material:

Taken from a moving bus somewhere between Dubno and Lvov, this
picture reveals a reversion to the ancestral way of building. The oldest part
of the building shows earthen construction with a straw roof, the next part
is earthen construction with a metal roof, and the newest part has earthen
walls and once again a straw roof.

Johann J. Gering, my wife's grandfather, made kiln-dried brick. Where he
learned this remains an enigma since he came from Volhynia, formerly in
Russia, where wood was plentiful and used freely in construction. His
American home of these bricks and the fence around it reveal a strong
Russian influence.

This house-barn combination built with Gering's kiln-dried brick was an exact duplicate of the home the Hofers left in Russia. The *Russian oven,* the barn and the porch over the entry were removed and a dormer was added. This is the David Hofer home near Freeman.

This is the same house as it looks a century later. It is presently occupied by a grandson of the builder, David Hofer.

Photographed in western Russia in 1973, this house still features the
principal characteristics of the 1874 homes in Dakota Territory.
Obviously the roof is not thatched and the method of heating is unknown.
But the house-barn combination, the vestibule by the door, the white
finish and heavy walls are motifs still much in evidence in the old homes
that still survive in Hutchinson County, South Dakota.

Nothing has been disturbed in this home since Mr. and Mrs. Lang moved
into a new home several years ago. Mr. Gottlieb Lang has a wealth of
information about building and living in rammed earth homes. His fondest
childhood recollection is that of coming home from church on a cold winter
Sunday and stepping through the door of the earthen home to the inviting
aroma of sauerkraut, potatoes and pork hocks simmering in the *Russian
oven*. For a long time the dirt floors in this home were sprinkled with sand.
Eventually wide boards were installed over the dirt and sand.

RAMMED EARTH — SEE DAVID MILLER.

Mr. J. Kleinsasser built this replica of his Russian home two miles west of Freeman. The ceiling beams were hauled from Yankton by oxen. Only three of the heavy timbers could be transported at one time. The thirty-four miles to Yankton and return required three days. No nails were used in the door and window frames. Everything was mortised and pegged with wooden pegs. However, Mr. Kleinsasser did bring nails from Yankton. These were driven into the earthen walls to give the stucco additional support.

This may look like a rock and concrete structure but the only cement used was in the basement and steps. The walls are rock and dirt. The Zanter House northwest of Freeman.

Lest I leave with you the impression that our ancestors lived like rodents in dirt mounds, let me present this Polish home. From 1800 to 1833 my Swiss ancestors lived in the general area of Poland where this house stands. In 1810 an event transpired in this home which has caused it to become a national shrine and an object of veneration. In that year a son was born to the family of lower middle class nobility that lived here. (The fine distinction in the social pecking order was defined by our Polish guide.) This son gained world renown as a foremost pianist. His name was Frederic Chopin. He was born to nobility and fame in a house similar to those built and occupied by our ancestors. Note the roof over the door, the protrusion at the corners and across the gable end, and the long, low lines of the roof and walls. There are thick walls and deeply recessed windows. This could just as well be the Elmer Grosz house in the Wittenberg area of Hutchinson County or any of the other earthern homes in South Dakota.

The birthplace of the renowned composer and pianist Frederic François Chopin (1810-1849). Born in Poland, he rose to fame in France.

Don't the exposed beams bring to mind Mr. Kleinsasser's three-day trips to Yankton with three heavy timbers? As you look at the wide floor boards, you again sense the joy Mr. Lang felt when similar boards were finally laid over the sand and dirt floors of his home. In a corner of the room stands a brick oven covered with ceramic tile. Surely it is fancier than the *Russian oven* prized by our ancestors, but still an earthen stove with the same attributes which excited the enthusiasm of Prentis and Butler.

Every time our guides showed us something that spoke to me of the homes of my ancestors, that happy little voice in my heart would shout its approbation. "It's a veritable monument. A monument to the industry of my forebears. A monument to their inventiveness and originality."

But that nagging voice in my head still isn't pacified. To this day it can be heard to grumble, "O.K. Nina. I'll grant you that you showed me more of the architecture of my ancestors than I had expected to see. But I must take exception to the words of your Nikolai Gogol. Like so many of your contemporary writers he states a basic truth and then proceeds to distort. Architecture is a chronicle of the world but it is not *"the chronicle.*" Without the legends and the songs and the poems its voice is inaudible. We Americans too have had writers who have addressed themselves to man's mortality and lasting value of the things he builds. Their statements may lack the romanticism of Gogol's pronouncements, but they certainly remain closer to the truth. One such man was writing when the patriarchs that built these homes were being born. Listen to his observations, Nina. Listen to our Washington Irving:

> "*Man passes away. His name fades from memory and recollection. His Life becomes as a tale that is told. His monument becomes a crumbling ruin.*" *Washington Irving's* Scrapbook.

Odyssey

This was the first speech given by Reuben Goertz after his Russia/Poland trip. Salem-Zion, North Church, Freeman, South Dakota, April 1973.

In 1874 my grandparents came from Russia with their parents. Although they had been born in Russia, they were not Russians; they were Germans. They settled on the Dakota prairie east of what is now Freeman, in homes very much like their neighbors and raised their families. My parents married in 1916 and homesteaded in Dawson County, Montana, and established a home similar to that of their neighbors.

I was born in a tar-paper shanty that was designed to be a granary after a permanent home could be built. In a frontier settlement where births and deaths were prime objects of conversation, my birth on the 7th of May, in 1918, went largely unnoticed. At the moment there was only one topic of conversation and that was—Reverend Franz, my minister, who only two weeks previously had been lynched for preaching in German to his little congregation of Germans from Russia. All part of a well-orchestrated program of constant harassment against all German-speaking people.

My parents returned to South Dakota, but relocation was not an escape. On the night of March 21, 1921, barricaded behind the tombstones in the Kaylor cemetery, a group of armed farmers and World War I veterans from Hutchinson County, held at bay a group of armed farmers and World War I veterans from Bon Homme County. The cause of the confrontation was a trainload of dairy cows that the Germans from Russia in Hutchinson County were sending to post-war Germany for humanitarian reasons.

These were not isolated cases. With distressing regularity, similar incidents were occurring from Kansas to Canada, wherever the Germans from Russia had settled.

IT WAS BECAUSE OF "GERMAN".

Who were these people who could generate so much suspicion and hostility? Where did they come from? What were their places of origin? Why did they leave their motherland? What were their migration routes? Why did they go to Russia? Why do they consider themselves German and not Russian? Where are they now?

These are the questions we will consider in this presentation.

First we will see how they were perceived by the established settlers of America's Midwest from Kansas to Canada. They aroused more ridicule than scorn. They elicited as much laughter as curiosity. Their simple homemade clothing gave them instant recognition and prompted Kansas news reporter Nobel Prentis to wryly inform the readers of the *Topeka Commonwealth*, "The men seem to have conscientious scruples against wearing clothes that fit them, the idea appearing to be to get all the cloth you can for the money. Their vests descend toward their knees and their pants possess an alarming amount of slack. Their favorite headgear appears to be a flat, black, cloth cap that they pull on in saluting everyone they meet—a habit they will soon forget now that they have arrived in Kansas where nobody respects nothing."

Dr. Hattie Plum Williams of the University of Nebraska is esteemed as the first American historian and sociologist to become interested in the Germans from Russia. Her master's thesis in 1909, entitled "The History of the German Russian Colony in Lincoln," begins with these words:

Standing on the corner of 10th and O streets in the city of Lincoln, any week-day morning between 7:30 and 8:00 o'clock, you may see pass by you from ten to twenty women with little black woolen shawls on their heads.

Ask any citizen who they are and ninety-nine times in one hundred he will tell you they are "Russians." As a matter of fact—his information is incorrect. These people, of whom there are about 4,000 in the city, are

Germans . . . not Russians. They are Teutons . . . not
Slavs. They are Lutheran and Reformed . . . not Greek
Catholics.

To be sure, they and their ancestors lived in Russia
for over 100 years, and they came here directly from the
realm of the Czar whose bona fide citizens they were;...
but they never spoke the Russian language, never
embraced the Greek religion, never intermarried with
the Russians, and many of their children never saw a
Russian until they left their native village for a new
home in America.

In Dakota Territory as elsewhere they were Russians in
print; out of print they were called Rooshuns or damnroo-
shuns. When the *Yankton Press and Dakotan* questioned the
Russians' rights to the use of the waiting rooms in the train
depot and described how the Russians make fuel from hay, it
was talking about Germans from Russia. My relatives and
friends would be very surprised to find out that the quaint
German dialect they learned from their parents was considered to be Russian by certain publishers. They were not
Russians but Germans from Russia.

So let us return to the place of origin of these people and
consider two things: 1) Why did they leave? 2) Why do they
insist they are German and not Russian?

The wide-open spaces of southwest Germany have
enticed the armies of Europe for centuries. Medieval infantry
battalions marched back and forth over their rolling hills.
Cavalry men charged about roughshod over the unobstructed
terrain. In the last two world wars the steel treads of tanks
have churned up the ground in combat.

Through the centuries, the harried peasants had the fruit
of their labors plundered and destroyed by both the advancing
and retreating armies. They were forced to pay confiscatory
taxes to support the pleasures of the nobility. Their sons were
recruited, not only for the nobleman's armed adventures, but

to be rented out to foreign governments as mercenaries, like the Hessians hired by the British in the Revolutionary War.

Even in our time this place continues as a playground for the gods of war. In an old trunk in the attic of a old home in my home town I found a picture of an ancestor in a Kaiser's uniform, mounted on a Kaiser's horse, conscripted to serve in the Kaiser's army. A century later his descendants returned to southwest Germany, their place of origin, in the uniforms of American doughboys to serve in yet another war. Another quarter of a century and this man's sons would return one more time in the uniform of an American G.I. to devastate the land in another conflict.

I have seen statistics of the casualties from the previous two centuries. They don't agree. It doesn't matter because they are so large I can't comprehend them anyhow. One set of figures says the population of this area was reduced from 16,000,000 to 2,000,000. Another set of figures is given as 18,000,000 to 3,000,000. Fourteen or fifteen million were killed or relocated. Hundreds of thousands went to Pennsylvania in the United States. About 3,300 families went east into Russia. They were the vanguard of a much larger group that would follow. They are the ones we are concerned about.

Because of the fickle fortunes of these many wars, boundary lines were changed. A part of Germany where some of my ancestors had lived and died now belongs to France. Some of my ancestors are buried in France. Not far from the French border is Weierhof, a village of historical significance to my people. We saw there a mix of old and new buildings that let us know there is no planned obsolesence in Weierhof. The sight of the old buildings was comforting because while I wonder if some of my forefathers lived in them, they speak to me of continuity and family.

The newer buildings in Weierhof were discomforting. They were some of the barracks of the United States Air Force. Their presence tells me that some people know that the threat of war that drove our people from this area centuries ago has

28,000 PEOPLE (?)

PRO-GERMAN PROPAGANDA

not yet been eliminated. While this knowledge saddens me, I am so thankful that my ancestors are numbered among those who had the foresight and courage to leave.

While we protest the name "Russians," the Germans try to set the record straight by hailing us as Germans. On the occasion of our America's bi-centennial in 1975, German Radio broadcast a series of programs out of Cologne to call attention to the German contributions to the development of America. They kept records of the people that left. They do not think of us as Russians; they consider us as Germans. They list the first group of immigrants to leave Germany and subsequent groups as well. The second group included the ancestors of Gen. George Armstrong Custer.

West of Freeman, my home town, is an area known as Heilbronn. The citizens of Heilbronn, Germany, have found five settlements scattered from Africa to Siberia inhabited by people whose roots are in Heilbronn, Germany, and whose settlements still bear the name Heilbronn.

The German Heibronners have published a book entitled *Heilbronn International*. In the chapter about Heilbronn, South Dakota, they deplore the fact that only a dirt road leads to Heilbronn in this state. A part of a South Dakota map like you have never seen is published in this book. They have penciled the location of Heilbronn on a South Dakota highway map. They have made it so prominent that it appears larger than Sioux Falls. Obviously they do not think of us as Russians; to the Germans we are Germans.

Many, many Germans from Russia can trace their ancestory to the Palatinate. *The Palatinate Homeland Greeting* is printed for and directed to those people scattered around the world whose ancestry can be traced to the Palatinate. One issue calls the attention of all of these people to my home town, the history of those citizens who trekked from the Palatinate to South Dakota and their part in a community celebration of our German-Russian heritage. They seem to be just as insistent as we are that we are German, not Russian.

In Weierhof there is a structure where my ancestors worshipped. The laws of the time prohibited the Mennonites from building churches; they were not allowed to erect steeples or have more than five families or twenty people worship together at one time. When the laws were liberalized, another building was constructed. Steeples were still not permitted, and they were still not allowed to call their place of worship a church. It was called a "Bethause" (House of Prayer), but it could be large enough to accommodate the entire congregation. It was built in 1837, but my ancestors never worshipped there. They had left for Russia forty years earlier. Those people that stayed paid a terrible price for the privilege.

Not far away is a house built, according to the inscription, by Michael Krehbiel in 1712. He named his place Primmerhof. Some of the Krehbiels from Primmerhof moved to Pennsylvania, Kansas, and South Dakota. Two Krehbiel families are members of my church in Freeman.

At the Primmerhof house, the Krehbiels all gathered in one doorway to greet us. The meeting was cordial because they recognize us as relatives. They do not think of us as Russians; they know we are Germans.

In my church in Freeman we have several families by the name of Miller. They can trace their roots to another little German church—the Ibersheim Church. The custodian of the church is also the custodian of the old church artifacts. He showed us an old Bible, possibly the pulpit Bible at the time my ancestors left there. It is four years older than Luther's Bible.

Many Americans now return to this part of Germany, not as soldiers but as researchers of their family histories, American citizens in search of some old questions. When the harried German burghers left Germany two centuries ago, why didn't they all go to America? Why did only some of them end up in Pennsylvania? Why were our grandparents born in Russia?

The German-born Czarina of Russia was responsible. She tempted the harried German peasants. She made them a promise that had all the seductive appeal of Eve's infamous apple. But her name wasn't Eve, and she wasn't Russian. She liked to be called Catherine the Great, but her name wasn't Catherine either. Her real name was Sophia Augusta; she wasn't Russian, and her greatness was hotly disputed.

At age thirteen she was a poverty-stricken German princess who arrived in Russia friendless and penniless with only three dresses to her name. She was married to the Grand Duke Peter, the heir to all the Russias. But Peter didn't amount to much. He would lie on the floor, for hours at a time, playing with wax dolls dressed in military uniform. He would go to bed with his boots on and spent much of his waking time in drinking. Catherine sustained herself by reading French authors and consoled herself by consorting with all manner of lovers.

It was not a happy or enduring marriage. He despised her, and she loathed him. He threatened to divorce her and to shut her up in a convent for life. She had one of her lovers put arsenic in his vodka. But he was surprisingly tough and the arsenic didn't kill him; so Catherine's lover knocked him down and choked him to death by thrusting a napkin down his throat. When we were in Russia, I asked our guide about this. She replied—"Napkin? heavens no, it was a stocking." Surely more gagging.

Then for thirty-four years after that, Catherine ruled over one of the greatest empires on earth. She never married again; but she wasn't exactly lonesome. For scores, yea, perhaps hundreds of different lovers, danced in the ballroom of her warm and romantic heart. She supported her lovers in regal splendor and squandered over five hundred million, pre-inflation, dollars on them. Yet she was so strict with her grandchildren that she made them stop studying botany when they started asking questions about the reproduction of plants.

Not very complimentary of Catherine

One of her favorites was an ugly giant named Potemkin. Potemkin only had one eye. He had lost the other in a tavern brawl. He went about his glittering palace with nothing on but house slippers on his bare feet. His hair was uncombed and he always needed a bath. He chewed his finger nails and ate raw onions and garlic. But Potemkin was a tornado of physical energy, and the mere touch of his hand filled Catherine with a vast and tender happiness. She called him her "golden pheasant," her pigeon, and her bow wow.

Although her bow wow trembled like a school girl whenever a cannon was fired, he was one of the greatest generals Russia ever had. He won a war with Turkey. As a prize of war he annexed a vast area of the defeated nation to Russia.

Catherine was so delighted that she built a palace for Potemkin. Potemkin was a compulsive gambler. One night he had a long run of bad luck at the gaming table and lost all of his money. In a desperate bid to recoup his losses, he bet the palace. He lost again. Catherine was so provoked she reclaimed the palace. When Catherine's son Paul became Czar, he used the building for a stable. He never had it cleaned, and it became the filthiest building in Russia. After the revolution the parliament (Duma) met here. Kerensky and his followers sat on the right side; Lenin and his mob sat on the left side, and ever since, your politics are considered either left or right of center.

In the south of Russia, the newly acquired Turkish land delighted Catherine. She would turn the vast steppes of the Ukraine into the breadbasket of the world, but to do this she needed good farmers to teach her backward serfs by example. She remembered the hard-working peasants in the Germany of her youth, and realized they were the people she needed.

She also wanted a foreign people to settle here as a buffer between her Russian subjects and the restive Turks. Her former countrymen would serve this purpose well. To entice these people into Russia she offered economic inducements— free land, tax exemption, and interest-free loans. But the

biggest attractions were military exemption and total auton-
omy in local government, churches, and schools.

The response of the German farmers was so overwhelm-
ing that within five years the German government passed laws
forbidding further emigration. The exodus could not be
stopped. The first years were difficult; many lives were lost.
The next generation fared better, and the third generation
prospered. As Dr. Stumpp has put it, the three generations can
be described in three words: Tot, Not und Brot. (Death,
Necessity, and Plenty). As the Germans prospered they built
banks.

The Germans were concerned about education and built
schools. The Chortitza Girls School, for example, still stands
and still serves as a school. But education here is served
through the benevolence of Lenin. The memory of the Germans
here has been deliberately obliterated. And the German-built
Central School in Halbstad (renamed Molochansk) was too nice
to be wasted on children and education. The city fathers now
use it for the Communist Party Headquarters.

We were anxious to see Berdyansk, a port city built on
the shore of the Sea of Azof to import the surplus wheat raised
by the Czar's Germans. After the revolution this ethnic group
was deliberately starved to death. This cruel form of genocide
was not practiced only on the adult male population. Countless
children were exterminated by deliberate starvation. The
worst famine in history took the lives of 20,000,000 people, as
many as were killed in Russia in World War II.

On the last day of our tour some of us were taken to
Berdyansk. We were told that only fourteen major buildings
built by the Germans remained. Schools and hospitals were
still being used for the purpose for which they were built.
Churches had their windows bricked shut. They are now
pressed into service as gymnasiums/auditoriums. The onion-
shaped domes on the Russian churches survived the revolution; the steeples on the German churches did not.

You may remember the Mennonites were not allowed to put steeples on their churches to begin with. So there was no steeple for the bolsheviks to tear down. They did destroy the fence, but one Mennonite church in Schoensee survived intact. But barely. The building is still being used, but not for its original purpose. It's full of sunflower seeds, presses to press out the oil, and barrels of sunflower oil.

A group of old people were standing about a ramshackle building in the mud and drizzle. Our question was answered when they piled into a truck to be taken to their assigned work place. As I watched them drive off, I realized again that if our ancestors wouldn't have had the courage to leave, and if by some miracle we had survived exile, starvation, and war, this would now be our lot. These were the lucky survivors.

Blauesfeld, Mariawohl, Gnadenthal, Morgenau—all were German villages that are now completely obliterated. Not one stone remains on another. The Russians have deliberately tried to erase all evidence that Germans ever lived here. Tombstones from German cemeteries have been incorporated into foundation walls and concrete steps. The cemetery sites were mostly plowed over. We found two graves that were overlooked.

On our last day in the Ukraine, the day some of us went to Berdyansk, some of the Russian-born members of our group got permission to take a taxi to the village of their birth. They went to the cemetery site to pay their respects to deceased elders. All that remained was an overgrown hole at the edge of the field where the cemetery had been. In the bottom of the hole they found a tomb stone. The inscription on the bottom bears the legend *Sanft ruhe Seine Asche* (Gently rest His Ashes). It was a lie. The grave had been violated. The ashes had been removed.

Alfonso Schulz was a refugee who came to Freeman after the war. He told how he was forced at bayonet point to exhume the bodies of his grandparents. The Bolsheviks then took the skulls and smashed them on the ground like so many ripe watermelon, looking for gold fillings in the teeth.

We visited the cemetery jungle in 1972, the second group of foreigners admitted since the revolution. The year before a group of twelve Canadians that had been born here were allowed to visit. When they passed this spot, they told their Intourist guide there should be a monument to a German-Russian hero on this spot. The bus was stopped and the monument and grave were located. The place the Canadians remembered was so overgrown they could hardly see it.

When the Russians gave us permission to come, they knew we too would want to see Heppner's Monument. So they cleaned it up for us, but they also told us the monument must go. They didn't care if it went to Canada or America or was dumped in the ocean, but go it must because they were going to turn this place into a shrine for the heroes of the Revolution, and every vestige and memory of the Germans must go. Some Canadian Germans from Russia raised the 5,000 rubles the Russians wanted for shipping charges. Now if you want to see Heppner's monument, you don't have to go to Russia. All you have to do is run up to Steinbach, Manitoba, about thirty-five miles this side of Winnipeg.

In all fairness it must be noted that the Germans had lived in Russia for one hundred years without becoming assimilated. They had prospered with special privileges not granted native Russians, and many had become elitists. This was an anomalous situation which could not last forever, and it didn't. The axe fell on June 4, 1871, when Alexander II issued a decree which repealed those provisions of the colonist code regarding local government and military exemption. The resultant shock waves rocked the German community. They were so agitated, it seemed the entire German population might move. The amazed Czar couldn't believe it and sent a personal emissary to reason with his aroused subjects.

General von Todleben was a personable man. The Germans liked him. By force of personality, his fluent command of the German language, and the power of his rhetoric he convinced 1.75 million Germans to accept the Czar's edict and to remain in Russia. A sizeable minority however was adamant and chose to leave Russia.

Churches sent delegations, primarily to America, to search out the best places to resettle. A photo is extant of the Mennonite delegation to Winnipeg in 1873. Not all the men on the picture are delegates. Since the biblical account of the Jewish scouts sent to Canaan specifically mentions twelve spies, Mennonites, who tend to interpret their Bibles literally, sent exactly twelve delegates. South America and even Australia were considered as future homes.

It was a historical coincidence of considerable consequences to the German colonists that just as Russia was abridging their privileges, several nations in the Americas were attempting to attract settlers by offering inducements reminiscent of those of Catherine. Earliest in the race was the United States. In 1862 President Lincoln signed the Homestead Act, which offered 160 acres of free land to any immigrant who indicated willingness to become an American citizen.

In the 1860's and '70's, American railway companies, endowed by their government with millions of acres of land, pushed their rails west across the great plains of the Midwest and their immigration propaganda east, across the ocean to the Germans in Russia. In the fall of 1872 the railroad from Sioux City penetrated the South Dakota border. In the early spring of 1873 the rails were laid to Yankton, and in March the first Germans from Russia came to Dakota Territory, hard on the heels of General Custer and his 7th Cavalry.

Since some of the land around Yankton was already taken, and the Germans wanted to settle in closed communities as they had in Russia, they pushed beyond the perimeter of the first settlements. Hutchinson County was still wide open, and they settled there and overflowed into adjacent parts of Turner, McCook, Douglas, Bon Homme, and Yankton

counties. By 1880 all available land in this area was filled with
Germans from Russia. The neighboring land had been infil-
trated by refugees and immigrants from other countries. Only
the northern tier of counties in South Dakota continued to
offer those vast regions so desirable for transplanting entire
communities from Russia. By now the railroad network had
extended to Aberdeen, and new immigrants ignored Yankton.
Eureka replaced Freeman as the Mecca for the new arrivals.
Alpena was established in 1883, Hosmer in 1884, and the list
goes on.

Since the individual German colonies in Russia were
originally settled with people of the same religious affiliation,
there were few interdenominational German villages in
Russia. They were either Catholic, Evangelical, or Mennonite,
and many of them bore the name of the ancestral village in
Germany. They tried to settle the same way in Dakota.

Since the railroad did not come to Hutchinson County till
1879, there were no towns; and once again the German settlers
tended to cluster in homogeneous groups bearing the names of
the places of origin in Germany. In the Freeman area to this
day the people, their dialects, their farms, and churches are
distinguished by names like Heilbronn, Kassel, KleinKassel,
Johannestahl, Wittenberg, etc. It has been said that the most
widely used German name in both Dakotas is Kulm. Kulm
township in Hutchinson County is too far west to fall into the
Freeman orbit.

States were settled in like manner. Kansas got mostly
Mennonites and Catholics. Nebraska and Colorado, the Volga
Germans, Reformed, and Lutheran. The Dakotas got the Black
Sea Germans, Protestant, and Catholic. Manitoba got mostly
Mennonites.

Few of the Old World traditions survive. Clannish isolation was swept away by intermarriage, education, the
outmigration of the young, and the loss of the German language. The various German dialects exist only in the homes of
those my age or older. The distinctive clothing survives only in

the Hutterite colonies. Traditional foods are eaten only on
festive occasions and at Schmeckfest.

It is difficult to fully gauge the impact of these people on
America. Because of suspicion, hostility, misunderstanding,
and the trauma of two wars with Germany, they have deliberately kept a low profile. They are not to be measured in terms
of outstanding individuals, but rather as a body of industrious,
conservative, highly patriotic people.

So where are we now? To me a photo of my grandson on
Ben Black Elk's lap best sums up our present situation. My
grandson certainly has the blood of two Germans-from-Russia,
Mennonite grandparents, flowing through his veins. But those
blonde features also reveal a Norwegian Lutheran grandfather, and the song in his heart betrays an Irish Catholic
grandmother. At this time all of that spiritual diversity is
being ecumenically blended in a Methodist church in Colorado.

As a fourth generation American, this child should find
his ethnic diversity to be a compelling reason to be a tolerant
and compassionate American. As the very red native American
gathers the very blonde child to his bosom, we have the
assurance that men of good will from all ethnic backgrounds
are striving to make the American dream come true for all
people. Maybe, at last, we have arrived at that place where
there will be validity in those old words that till now have had
a ring of hollow mockery about them:

> Lord, set all thy people free
> From foolish rivalry.
> Set all free.
> Let all past bitterness now and forever cease,
> And all our souls possess,
> True charity.
> Forgive, O Lord, our severing ways.
> The rival altars that we raise.
> The wrangling tongues that mar thy praise.
> Dear Lord forgive.

Wedding Bells Ringing, Skeletons in Closets Jingling

This article is based on a slide presentation made by the author at the Fifth International Convention of the American Historical Society of Germans from Russia in Fresno, California, June 20, 1974.

The first marriage in Dakota Territory conducted according to the legal forms then recognized occurred on the first day of January, 1859, at the house of Louis St. Onge, on Big Sioux Point in Union County, according to an early issue of the *Press and Dakotian.*

The groom was John Claude, and the bride a dusky maid of the forest and a relative of the St. Onge family. The ceremony was performed by John H. Charles, then a justice of the peace of Sioux City. He was assisted in the ceremony by Enos Stutsman, Yankton pioneer, who "made a prayer, sang a song and delivered a lecture to the newly wedded couple which, coming from a bachelor, contained some astounding statements and advice in which he did not appear to consider the physical endurance of the groom." The account continues:

After the ceremony dancing commenced to the squeaky music of a cheap fiddle in the hands of a negro named John Brazeau, who lived with the indians, and whose boast it was that he was "de fust white man who built a house in Dakota Territory." At a late hour the festivities ceased, and the party adjourned to a neighboring cabin where a feast had been prepared. The appetite of the guests had been sharpened by the vigorous exercise of swinging a 200 pound squaw through the rapid and muscular changes of a Big Sioux cotillion, and all partook most heartily of the viands set before them, and it was not until after their hunger was fully appeased, and they took time to examine the appearance of the remnants before them, that the truth fastened upon their minds that dog meat was not all unsavory.

Although this was the first marriage in the Territory under a quasi-legal ceremony, it did not prove a happy or enduring one. At the end of two weeks the bride deserted her husband and returned to the parental tepee, alleging as an excuse for her action the astounding assertation that she could not sleep with her husband because his feet gave forth an odor directly the opposite of the exhalations of the night-blooming cereus.[1]

This was only fifteen years before the Germans from Russia started invading Dakota Territory in substantial numbers. Now wedding became *Hochzeit,* the justice of peace relinquished his role to the *Prediger,* and *Schinken Fleisch* curried favor over canine meat as the table delicacy. Otherwise very little was changed. Carried away by the exuberance of the festive occasion an occasional German indiscreetly dropped his usual reserve. In soberer moments he had ample opportunity to repent since friend and foe would not let him forget things he might not even remember. We cannot ring the old wedding bells too vigorously lest we jingle a family skeleton or two moldering in some musty closet.

The format for wedding celebrations changed little, but the path to the altar has seen more changes than you see fluttering on the clothesline of a home with a tiny infant. Let's examine a few.

Before the turn of the century an arranged marriage was universally accepted. It was approved by all except some of the young couples involved. We know of instances where young men and women did not relinquish their unmarried status cheerfully, in a romantic aura of love and kisses. They did not like to have their marriage contracted for the sake of propriety, propagation and property rights.[2] Not much has been said about this. More exposure has been given to those who were too cheerfully romantic without matrimony than those unhappy in a bleak marriage void of love. Unlike the 1859 wedding, these unions were binding. Divorce was unheard of in spite of the lack of love or inattention to personal hygiene.

The casual approach to such an important event is best illustrated by a case history in my community. The names of the characters have been changed to protect me from their irate progeny.

Herr and Frau Schwartz decided by whatever methods parents arrived at such decisions that son Jakob was ready for matrimony. Once this was agreed upon there remained the matter of "who?" Of the marriageable young maidens in the community the young daughter of Christian Weisz seemed the logical choice. With this problem resolved, the *Stöckelmann* (marriage broker) was summoned, apprised of the situation and asked for his services.

As he was wont to do, the *Stöckelmann* readily agreed, but he had one request. Since the *Stöckelmann* lived in Freeman and the Weisz family lived at the far side of the community, the ride out and back would be long and lonely. Would the Schwartzes mind if he took a friend along to while away the weary hours? The Schwartzes were agreeable and on the morning of the next day the *Stöckelmann* and his crony set out for the Weisz homestead with team and buggy.

The early morning hours held forth the promise of an extremely hot day. The sun slipped over the horizon as a searing orb in a cloudless sky. Bird songs were stifled in parched throats by the oppressive heat. Dust raised by the horses' hooves and buggy wheels hung thick and motionless in choking clouds. The two couriers in the buggy agreed that it was going to be a hot day indeed. Even at a slow walk it was unlikely that the team would be able to endure the trip to the Weiszes and back. At this rate they would be only by Grosze Heinrich at noon. When they should be turning homeward, they would be only slightly over half way to the Weisz farm.

They would water and rest the horses by Grosze Heinrich while they joined their family for dinner and then decide whether to go on or return home.

Suddenly the *Stöckelmann* was jolted from his lethargy by the birth pangs of a new and wondrous idea. Grosze Heinrich had not one but three daughters of marriageable age. Not only were they blessed with good health, they were large and able to work long and hard. Their piety could be taken for granted for theirs was a religious family. Wasn't Grosze Heinrich even a *Vorsinger* in the church? The only imaginable blemish with this plan would be an unwarranted objection by Herr and Frau Schwartz. Surely they too must realize what a hot day this is.

Grosze Heinrich received his unexpected guest graciously. The horses were watered and fed while two extra places were set at the table. Grosze Heinrich and his wife commiserated with their guests as they told of the difficulties imposed on their mission by this unusual heat. Both commended the *Stöckelmann* most heartily on the wisdom of his newest inspiration. Thus encouraged, the travelers aborted their journey and returned to the Schwartzes. The Schwartzes were reasonable people and agreed that in the unprecedented heat the *Stöckelmann* had acted wisely. As a consequence the gentleman that just recently retired from the highest elective office in Hutchinson county had a Grosze Heinrich daughter for a mother instead of a Weisz.

To be the beneficiary of this age-old tradition you had to have a family to look after your welfare and do the arranging. A substantial number of young men, forsaking parents and fatherland, came to America alone. Bereft of parental intercessors they had to rely on their own ingenuity to find a wife in the matrimonial market place. A court of last resort for these underprivileged swains was the "lonely hearts" column, common in many papers. This gave the candidates the widest possible exposure. We know of at least two young men (one of them a great uncle of mine) who enticed brides from Germany

to relocate in Dakota Territory under the protective benevolence of these reticent Romeos. Both unions were blessed with
many children and various other accoutrements of a happy
marriage and all spoke proudly of their "mail order" spouses.
In the neighboring town of Marion the local editor
printed a list of eligible bachelors, not as a paid advertisement
but as a public service. The February 19, 1880, edition of the
Marion *Gazette* carried the following announcement:

> Letter to the marriageable young ladies of Turner
> County:
> This being leap year, and as the young men of this
> town are noted for their native modesty, taken in connec-
> tion with the fact that nearly, if not quite all, are new
> comers, and perhaps have not had the opportunities to
> become acquainted with you, we say, that in view of the
> facts as above stated, we deem it our duty to present to
> your notice the names of the young men in Marion and
> vicinity who are now in the matrimonial market. They
> are as follows . . . .

The editor listed thirty-six names, including that of Jacob
Hieb, grandfather of Dr. Bill Hieb of Henderson, Nebraska.
The editor was dumbfounded when brickbats instead of
accolades were the indignant response from his would-be
beneficiaries. Before physical violence could render our
misguided cupid speechless, an unknown lady got him off the
hook with a letter of reply. In the March 11 issue of the Marion
Gazette the editor could gloat,

> . . . a short time ago we published a list of the marriage-
> ble young men in town. Some of the boys were mad
> enough to eat two eggs, but they won't be mad any more
> when we tell them that last week one of the young men
> whose name was published in that list, received a letter
> written in a dainty feminine hand which reads about in

this wise: "You will pardon the liberty I take in addressing you, but I saw your name in a list of marriageble
young men, published in the Marion *Gazette* (sent me by
a friend) a few days ago, and as this is leap year, I claim
the privilege of a correspondence. I am considered good
looking, am moral, and respectably connected. If you
deign to answer this, I will in my next give to you my
true name and address."[3]

Unfortunately a fire destroyed the Marion *Gazette* and all
the files shortly thereafter, and we do not know the ultimate
outcome of the above incident. Neither do we know the cause
of the fire. Was it ignited by the volatile contents of the torrid
love letters instigated by the editor's benevolence? Or could
the ruffled dispositions of the thirty-five boys whose names
were printed but whose indignation was not mollified by a
feminine response have been a contributing factor?

The winds that whipped the flames that consumed the
Marion *Gazette* also wafted a hint of change to wary parents
and whispered the hope of better ways to the young. Since the
German equivalent of puppy love and moonstruck is missing
from my limited German vocabulary I can only assume the
silly antics suggested by these phrases are purely American
expressions born at the time these young Germans wrested
their matrimonial destiny from their parents. True, "*Er hat
Heiratsgedanken*" excused an occasional lapse of memory but
had none of the connotations of the absurd behavioral aberra-
tions brought to mind by puppy love.

Instead of relying on parents, piety and productive work
to provide a helpmate, the young now strove to make themselves as attractive as possible. One of the first citadels of
conservative symbolism to fall among my people was the basic
black, unadorned clothing. Improving economic conditions on
the frontier certainly served the youth well in their cultural
revolution. One old patriarch glumly observed,

Doch mit den bessern Verhältnissen kam auch der Sinn sich zu schmücken. Schön—und Einfachkeit ist ja eine Tugend: aber das war nicht immer in der Gesinnung der Putsüchtigen. Steife Kragen und Handlinten, Schleifen, Uhrketten, und bei den Frauen die mehrmal aufgekrausten Kleider, Hüte mit federn oder Blumenschmuck und dergleichen mehr, wurde scheinbar zur Notwendigkeit, welches Anlasz zu allerlei Streit und Uneinigkeiten gab. "Stellet euch nicht dieser Welt gleich"[4] und "Ihr Schmuck soll nicht auswendig sein"[5] waren zutreffende Schrifstellen, womit man seine meinung begründete.[6]

With the better conditions came the tendency to preen oneself. Nice and simple is a virtue but this was not always uppermost in the minds of the vain. Stiff collars and cuffs, neckties, watch chains and frequently by the ladies ruffled clothes, hats adorned with feathers or flowers and the like seemed a necessity which led to all manner of strife and disunion. "Be not conformed to this world" and "That women adorn themselves in modest apparel, with shamefacedness and sobriety" were appropriate scriptures on which these precepts were founded.

The ladies were quicker than the men to change the style of their attire drastically. Every knowledgeable girl tried to dispel the old image of being frugal, formless and fertile. They now strove mightily to appear available, attractive and amorous. In searching for the most attractive combination of guile and dress they began experimenting with their apparel, a custom that continues to this day.

One innovation that happily didn't last too long was the bustle, also known as the "Deceitful Seatful." Today we might call it the watergate: so much is suggested, so little revealed. A large undercover operation is indicated but everything is obscured by a massive coverup.

Proper ladies in prim suits were more attractive. What the bustle had formerly done to attract attention to one end of the anatomy the large new hats did for the other end. These hats too were an enigma. The venturesome female wore them to attract and repel. Designed to lure, those horrendous brims would then keep the ardent swain at a virtuous distance. They also sheathed those long pins which kept both hats and boys in place. The negative aspects of this arrangement must have outweighed the positive too heavily. Again the members of the fairer sex amended their method of exciting interest.

Like the bustle, the immense hat was jettisoned. Caution was thrown to the winds and the hemlines began to creep up. This trend too continues to this day but is expected to stop shortly; the end is already in view. Dainty ankles, ensconced in pointed button shoes, were revealed. Heavy materials in subdued colors gave way to white translucent materials woven of the gossamer fabric of angel wings. As always the boys were amendable to change. Smirked one whose German had been as corrupted as his will to resist,

> *Repress ich so a Wish für sinful Action,*
> *Da glowt mei Herz mit inner Satisfaction.*
> *But, bin ich unsuccessful in restraining*
> *Das Beast in mir, ist's auch ganz entertaining.*[7]

For their part, the young men were quite content with their clothes. Their choice of clothing did not gyrate as wildly as it did with the distaff members of society. Trouser legs did vary in their tightness. Starched and celluloid collars came and went. Watch chains became a status symbol. But mostly men were content with one good Sunday suit. Their situation was much improved from that of one pioneer grandfather who had so few clothes that he thought to change for church meant to turn his trousers inside out to present the cleanest side to the congregation.

This casual attitude toward clothing does not indicate a lack of interest in the mating game. The men directed their energy and financial resources to the acquisition of fine horses, buggies, sleighs, motorcycles and finally cars. Excellence and elegance in transportation became an obsession with the young, a perpetual concern with the parents. The advent of the automobile doomed all the old courting traditions in one full swoop. Mobility offered escape from confinement and surveillance. Parents haven't known the whereabouts of their children since.

Although the rapidly changing mores may be blamed on the car and provocative styles, the end result was the same as when the feet were the only means of locomotion and a modestly draped fig leaf the only method of hiding one's gender. The forces unleashed by Eve's guile and Adam's curiosity inexorably ground on to their ultimate destiny. Sooner or later the young people decided to get married.

There wasn't time for a protracted romance. The German girl's capacity for hard manual labor in addition to her housekeeping skills made her a valuable asset to any aspiring young farmer. The appellation "old maid" was scrupulously avoided by all the young girls. After the sixteenth birthday the spectre of impending spinsterhood weighed heavily on daughter and parents alike. The powers of nature, society and practical economics exerted constant pressure for an early marriage. After the couple succumbed to these forces there loomed one terrifyng hurdle.

The trauma of this ordeal cooled the fires of passion to a mere glow in many a prospective groom. Now, in retrospect the *Stöckelmann* did not seem like such an archaic relic of the stone age. Many trembling matrimonial candidates would gladly have paid a king's ransom for his services now. In the absence of the official matchmaker the young man must now make his own plea to the parents for their daughter's hand. Hat in hand, heart in throat, the young man presented himself to a stern father who always managed to be taken by surprise.

From the academic questions posed by the father one could only assume that he and his daughter had not communicated in years. Before the inquisition rendered the boy entirely insensible the father relented and events now quickly rushed to their culmination.

The engaged couple now went to the minister, ostensibly to ask him to officiate at the wedding and to reserve the church for the chosen time. In this small community word of their engagement had surely preceded them and their visit came as no surprise to the pastor. It did give the man of the cloth the opportunity to offer a few little homilies about the virtuous wife, the faithful husband and the influence of the Christian home on those little children expected in rapid succession.

The church janitor was probably the only person favored with a personal invitation. One young couple that overlooked this bit of protocol had ample reason to rue their indiscretion. When they and the guests arrived at the church, which was always open, the door was locked. The janitor was absent. A messenger was dispatched to summon him. The janitor insisted that he was ignorant of the entire affair.

Preparing the guest list at that time was not the harrowing experience it is today. Since you both grew up in the same community, were of the same faith and related to practically everyone, and since those not invited would shivaree with a vengeance at a later date, you simply invited everybody and the janitor.

Because the wedding celebration was a lavish affair, sometimes lasting two days, it was a matter of financial expediency to have as many couples marry at one time as possible. Double weddings were commonplace. The largest wedding in our community involved five couples. The work and people involved in the preparation staggers the imagination.

Mrs. Alfred Waltner, the widow of a former minister, wrote the following account. Mrs. Waltner is eighty-five years old. She was married in a double ceremony but well remembers some of the larger weddings. Mrs. Waltner would rather write in German but has graciously submitted the following report in English. The comments in parenthesis are mine:

When a couple was ready to get married the matter had to be talked over with the parents. Plans were made, the day set and meals planned. When there were three, four or five couples, that sure was a big wedding involving lots of planning and much work.

Groom and bride had to go to town and buy the material for her wedding dress so she would have plenty of time to make it. Usually she had help.

As time went on relatives and neighbors were asked to mark their dishes, knives and forks, teaspoons and tablespoons.

Sawhorses had to be made. Big ones for the tables and little ones for the benches. (Barrels and nail kegs were also used for the same purpose.) Also lumber had to be gotten from the lumber yard for the tables and benches.

Often a building like a machine shed was cleaned to put up the tables. Later some put up tents. (When the trees planted by the first pioneers got big enough, tables were set under the trees if the weather permitted.)

The day before the wedding fathers were busy with butchering, mostly beef. (For a quadruple wedding in 1906 three beeves were butchered.) Mothers, girls and relatives were busy with baking bread, pie, cake and cookies. A lot of them! Somebody was asked to bake the wedding cake. Sauce usually was made of dry apple-schnitz and what goes with it. Plums, peaches and apricots were added to give a good taste. Often a big crock full. Potatoes were peeled the day before and kept in washtubs. Some mother was asked to take over the responsibility for the meal, to see that all was done well.

Wedding morning everybody got up early. Chores had to be done and many things to get ready.

Meat was cooked in big kettles; coffee and potatoes in washboilers. There was some kind of vegetable, often sauerkraut.

Coming to church the pastors took the lead. Each couple had two side couples. No wedding march. When there were two, three or four and five couples that was a long procession. One pastor made the "einleitung," the other gave the sermon. Not only a sermonette—all together maybe an hour and a half. With singing from Gesangbuch and Evengelium's Buch coming into the church and leaving the church. The same tempo.

Coming to the home, tables were set and the wedding guests were seated around the tables. One of the pastors prayed and also here, in a special way, asked God's blessing upon the newlyweds for material blessings as well as spiritual blessings. *Dann lieszen die hochzeitgäszte es sich gut schmecken.*

Afternoon was spent in visiting (Dancing was strictly *verboten* by our church.)

No honeymoon trip.

The following day was clean up day.[8]

Being a minister's wife, Mrs. Waltner felt she could not in good conscience address herself to the matter of alcoholic beverages served at weddings. I have no desire to detract from her recollections by injecting my own pungent observations at this point.

I do not recall these incidents to laugh at my forefathers but rather to laugh with them. We know these stories and events only because they themselves told and retold them. Aware of their shortcomings and inconsistencies, they didn't dwell on them, but by chiding one another they helped each other strive after their ultimate destiny.

1. *Yankton Press and Dakotan:* 1936 edition (Diamond Jubilee Celebration of Creation of Dakota Territory at Yankton. 75th Anniversary of *Yankton Press and Dakotan.*)

2. Nina Farewell, *Every Girl is Entitled to a Husband,* New York, 1963, p. 9.

3. Reprinted in the Marion (South Dakota) *Record,* July 29, 1954.

4. I Timothy 2:9.

5. Romans 12:2.

6. P. R. Kaufman, *Unser Volk und Seine Geschichte,* 1931.

7. K. M. S., *Die Allerschönste Lengevitch.* New York, 1953, p. 106.

8. Anna Waltner, unpublished manuscript, 1974.

d good

An Irreverent Mennonite Casts Sidelong Glances at His Volga Compatriots

Published in the Journal of the American Historical Society of Germans from Russia *1.3 (Winter 1978): 23-27.*

Two little toddlers, a Catholic boy and a Protestant girl, were playing by a mud puddle. They became thoroughly soaked. To avoid censure from their parents they disrobed to dry their clothes in the sun before returning home. Observed the little girl, "I always knew there was a difference between Catholics and Protestants but I never knew there was so much difference!"

I, too, have suffered from an immoderate curiosity about a difference . . . the real difference between the Mennonites and the Volga Germans. This aura of curiosity did not extend to the Black Sea Germans. I had been surrounded by them from the time of my earliest memories. Continued proximity had stripped the mantle of mystery, and I found most of their life styles more compatible with mine than those of the more divergent groups of fellow Mennonites.

The Volga Germans were *eine andere Sache.* They had not intruded on my consciousness until I joined The American Historical Society of Germans from Russia. To this day their dialect demands my full attention if I'm to get the gist of what they are saying. Their odd names for ethnic foods keep me guessing what I'm going to eat until the dish is set before me. In agriculture they relate to sugar beets instead of wheat. Instead of paying homage to Molotchna and Chortitza and the Black Sea and Crimea and Odessa, they prattle on about Wiesenseite and Bergseite and Saratov and Frank. Truly a different people. Probably a devious people. Those superficial differences which they allow to surface in casual social intercourse seemed carefully contrived to mask much more fundamental differences lurking beneath the surface. What are the basic differences between the Mennonites and the Volga Germans?

I was able to fathom the differences in South America. Once ensconced in a Volga German home, I asked questions and made my own observations without the promptings and explanations of my traveling companions. I exercised my peripheral vision by practicing sidelong glances. These oblique glances were intended to be all encompassing and inconspicuous. My wife noticed at once and accused me of becoming a lecherous old man with a roving eye. Having an attractive young girl like Barbara in our group did nothing to allay her fears. I remained adamant in my resolve and would like to share a few of the observations gleaned from my questions and sidelong glances.

The bus braked to a stop in front of a modest stucco home pressing against the sidewalk in Crespo calle Rivadavia, 1655 Entre Rios, Argentina. Jimmy and I heard our names called and were the first of our group to retrieve our luggage and join our South American hosts. David and Amalia Schmidt, Volga Germans of the Evangelical Lutheran persuasion, shook our hands and invited us into their home. The quiet reserve of the initial meeting quickly mellowed as we became acquainted and felt the fellowship of a common heritage.

The stucco home was four years old. It and much of the furniture in it was built by the Schmidts when they retired from their farm. The home and the garden behind it were meticulously cared for by the industrious *Hausfrau*. With undisguised pride the Schmidts let it be known that the bulk of their diet was provided by their farm and garden. Their children on the farm always brought fresh dairy products and other farm produce when they came to town. Just like any well-ordered Mennonite family.

We were asked about our church affiliation.When we replied we were Mennonites, there was a slight pause, a quizzical look and a forthright admission that they had heard of such but never seen any. That dismissed the topic of religion. Religion per se was not discussed again, but the deep faith and obvious convictions of these people soon gave me to know that with the exception of some external methods I would find no great difference between these pious Volga Germans and a devout Mennonite family in the matter of faith.

Invited to supper we were ushered into a small but cozy kitchen. The fare was simple but nourishing. Mrs. Schmidt held a large loaf of homebaked bread against her bosom and cut off thick slices. Homemade butter and jams made the German pastries on the table superfluous. Cups of steaming hot coffee beckoned. Before we could partake, heads were bowed and hands were folded as Mr. Schmidt prayed:

Komm, Herr Jesu, Sei unser Gast
Und segne alles
Was Du uns besheret hast, Amen.

When Mennonite children still spoke German in the home, this prayer was the one they learned as soon as they could cope with something longer than

Aba, Lieber Vater, Amen.

Sunday morning breakfast featured fresh orange juice squeezed from home-grown oranges and a food that used to be very popular with the Volhynian Swiss (my people). To my knowledge it was not enjoyed by other Mennonite groups. This delicacy was *Fauler Köse*. Mrs. Schmidt said some also called it *Gekochter Köse*. This took me back in time to my mother's table when I was still at home. Though Jimmy enjoys it and would like to make it, her culinary activities are curtailed by the lack of homemade cottage cheese. The cultured cottage cheese available in our supermarkets may be fine for calorie counters but does not lend itself to the making of *Fauler Köse*. Sunday dinner started with homemade chicken noodle soup. It looked and tasted like Mennonite noodle soup. Chicken meat, pan-fried beef, and canned home-grown peaches rounded out the meal. I was content . . . . I was in my element.

Never were we asked if we wanted to go to church. It was assumed that all good Germans from Russia go to church on Sunday morning. Like Scrooge with the spirit of Christmas past, I was suddenly confronted with my younger years. In 1931 I started catechism. This moved me from the front pews on the men's side (little girls sat on the women's side) to the catechism class. The battle of the language was raging in the congregation. Some evening services and an occasional Sunday morning hymn were in English. The rest was all in German. The change to English was inevitable. Ours was the only catechism class that was ever offered a choice of German or English. Soon there would be one English worship service a month, then two, and finally all Sunday morning services were English with an occasional German hymn and infrequent German services in the evening. Grandmother was heartbroken.

Now in 1978, in South America in an Evangelical Lutheran Church, I sat on the men's side, far removed from my wife, who was somewhere across the aisle surrounded by the distaff members of the congregation. On the front benches, giggling girls on the women's side were exchanging coy glances with the restless boys on the front benches on the men's side. In this church, services alternate between German and Spanish on a weekly basis. This was the Spanish Sunday. I couldn't fault the Volga Germans for the intrusion of this strange language. I had been in Mennonite churches in Alsace where my people (Grabers, Kaufmans, Schrags, etc.) now worship in French. *Das Volk auf dem Weg* has found refuge in many strange havens.

The crosscurrent of vague memories roused from a somnolent past, crashing against strange Spanish sounds in an old church in a foreign land induced an eerie reverie. An irretrievable past was confronting an uncertain future. I sat back and let the sounds and atmosphere engulf me and my thoughts as the Spanish droned on.

The intrusion of spoken German in the Spanish service propelled me back to the present. In observance of the centennial, the services would close with a German song. Not a familiar old hymn but an *Auswanderungs Lied*. I sat bolt upright. I was wide awake. How had my Volhynian Swiss *Auswanderungs Lied* found its way to the Volga German settlement in provincial South America? A quick glance at the mimeographed sheets handed us showed it was not the same song. The Volga version was written by a certain Andreas Richert. The Mennonite song was written by Elder Jacob Stucky in Kotosufka, Zshitomir District, in Volhynia on July 30, 1874.* The first two groups of my people had already departed from Russia. Elder Stucky would follow in another month with the remainder. Other Mennonite groups have laid vague claims to the song.

In the April 9, 1974, issue of *Der Bote* a Mr. D. J. Friesen (Low German) of Abbotsford, B. C., writes of his leaving Russia in 1924, *"Da zur damaligien Zeit noch wenige ans Auswandern dachten, sang meine liebe Frau unseren kleinen Kindern, Mariechen und David, ein Auswander lied vor, welches sie bald auswendig konnten und den Tag über sangen:*

Jezt ist die Zeit und Stunde da,
Wir ziehen nach Amerika. etc. etc. (The Elder Stucky song)."

David Hofer, the oldest resident of the Wolf Creek Hutterite colony, was visiting in our home and insinuated it was a Hutterite song. When he started to sing it my wife hid the tape recorder under a cloth covering some freshly baked bread. (Hutterites are opposed to recordings and picture taking.) The battery on the recorder was old and the tape dragged. Now when we play it at a normal speed, old David sounds like a high soprano trilling along in high gear. He sang a different melody than my people use, but the words, even after being strained through a cloth, are familiar:

> *Jezt ist die Zeit und Stunde da,* etc. etc.

Now the Volga Germans have a song that not only traces the *Auswanderung* from Russia in the eighteen seventies, but goes back to the *Auswanderung* from Germany more than a century before. I imagine, however, that the song is one of retrospect and was written much later. The date of the song is not given.

The song by Richert uses nine verses to trace the wanderings of the Volga Germans. They leave Germany:

> *Die Alte Heimat war zu enge,*
> *Es fehlt das täglich Brot im Haus,* etc. etc.

They arrive by the Volga:

> *Man Eilte, eilte Wochen, Tage,*
> *recht tief ins weite grosse Land,*
> *bis man am Wüsten Wolgastrande*
> *für sich ein kleines Plätzchen fand.* etc. etc.

The next three verses tell of overcoming pioneer hardships and establishing a good life on the Volga. Verse six tells of the beginning of the end:

> *Die ew'ge Freiheit ist zu Ende,*
> *die Katharine ihnen bot.*
> *Das Wandern, Wandern nimmt kein Ende!*
> *Wohin? Das weiss allein nur Gott . . .* etc. etc.

The last three verses are a song of thanksgiving for deliverance from Russia:

Wir preisen ihn von ganzem Herzen, etc. etc.

The choir was instructed to sing the first two verses in unison to acquaint the congregation with the melody. Then the entire assembly was to join in the last seven verses. The first bars of the melody jolted all thoughts of active participation from my mind. That tune! What was the name of that tune? What was the name of that haunting tune? It was like an old familiar friend, but I couldn't remember where I had heard it or the name of it. The choir had finished the first two verses. I knew what every note would be before they sang it, but the name eluded me. The intensity with which the people sang made it imperative that I name that tune. It eluded me. The song was almost finished; only a few verses remained. I was getting frantic when all of a sudden it came to me. I was overwhelmed. For with the name of the melody came the realization that I had just stumbled on a bit of folklore common to my Mennonite ancestry and the Volga Germans.

Larisa, our Intourist guide, was standing on the shore of Chortitza Island, on the spot where the first Mennonites had settled in Russia. She was explaining how the immense rocks protruding above the churning waters of the Dnieper River long had been the only means of access to the island unless you had a boat. Unless the boat was very large, it was an extremely hazardous way to get to the island. For this reason the island had been a bastion for bands of Cossacks. As she was telling the legends of the various rocks (Rock of Lovers, Rock of Fools, Rock of Moans and Groans, The Kettle Rock, etc. etc.) it seemed to me I had heard this all before. I asked Larisa, "This wouldn't be the island where Stenka Razin was married?" Larisa was dumbfounded. "You know about Stenka Razin?" Now it was my turn to use her favorite expression, "Oh yes! But of course." She assured me that this was indeed the island where Stenka Razin was married. Thereby hangs a tale.

Stenka Razin was the Russian Robin Hood. He ranged up and down the Volga River exacting tribute from merchant caravans and larger settlements. He was born in 1513, which means Stenka Razin was raising havoc in the land that would one day be populated by people whose stay in Germany would be made untenable by the consequences of the Reformation that was tearing Europe asunder during this time. As his power and reputation grew, so did the extent of his range. He roamed far from his power base of the Volga. When he was quartered on the island fortress of Chortitza (where one day my people would settle), he took a wife and brought her on this island where no women were allowed. No one dared challenge this indiscretion of this powerful leader. But in the morning when he emerged from the nuptial tent he stood alone. During the night all his men had moved across the river. Stenka Razin put his new wife in a boat and rowed to the middle of the river and called to his men. When he had their attention he stood up in the boat and in his powerful hands held his bride of one night high above his head. In full view of all he threw her into the river and watched as she drowned.

His men cheered his heroism and once again rallied about him. To this day Stenka Razin remains a Russian hero. His is the third picture on the ceiling of the Hall of National Heroes in the Moscow metro. He gets prominent attention in the Russian encyclopedias. Above all, what must be one of the most beautiful folk songs in all of Russia keeps the story of Stenka and his bride alive. Larisa took me to the record shop and helped me find a record of the Red Army Chorus singing this haunting melody. I still have the score, an eight-part arrangement, that some of us sang in an American Army male chorus. And this was the tune I heard in an Evangelical Lutheran church in Argentina as the people sadly sang of a lost fatherland on the Volga of Stenka Razin.

Between spoons full of noodle soup I asked Mr. Schmidt
if the Volga Germans ever practiced _Hexerei_ or _Zauberei_. This
question was prompted by a letter I have at home from an
eighty-five-year-old man in Canada. He left our community in
Freeman, South Dakota, as a young man. The following is an
excerpt from a letter he wrote about his memories of my
community:

> When my brother Andrew who died from diphtheria
> later, was about ten years old, a kind of rash formed on
> his chin up to his lower lip. Mother treated it but it
> didn't heal so the parents decided to take him to a Mr.
> Albrecht who lived about four miles north towards
> Marion. [One of this Albrecht's sons married one of my
> father's sisters, another son married one of my mother's
> sisters.] He was known to cure ailments by incantation
> (_Absprechen_) in German. I went along; . . . after greet-
> ings Albrecht had Andrew sit in front of him facing each
> other; then Albrecht began to whisper as if saying a
> silent prayer. Then he stopped, bent forward, puckered
> his lips and kept blowing into the sore for several
> breaths, then changed off to whispering something again.
> He kept this procedure up for about six rounds. Then he
> said to my father, "Take the boy home, the sore will
> heal." And sure enough, the next morning it looked like
> it was beginning to heal and within a week the sore was
> full healed! I wonder was that divine or sort of occult
> healing? . . . some of our people firmly believed in
> witchcraft!

From folklore sessions at previous conventions I knew
that the Volga Germans in America had some fascination with
the mystique of the supernatural, but I couldn't fathom the
depths of their indulgence. Maybe South America would offer
a clue. I hadn't anticipated ths vehemence of Mr. Schmidt's
reply:

"Did they?" He replied in the most agitated voice I ever heard this mild-mannered man use. "They still do!" he exploded. He explained that as the doctor's fees escalate, more and more people are turning to the occult for healing. Less than two blocks from his home, right on the road to the church, lives a woman who boasts such power, and more and more people are turning to her. The church does not sanction this and has published a pamphlet warning of the dire consequences. He got up from the table and left the room. When he returned he had one of the pamphlets which he handed to me. This is probably my most prized souvenir of the South American trip. It has as complete an inventory of the various methods of *Aberglauben und Zauberei* as I have ever seen. I'll give the title and a few pertinent quotes.

EINE GEFÄHRLICHE UNWISSENHEIT!
Kurzgefaszte biblische Aufklärung über Aberglauben und Zauberei
Wer dem Glauben die Tür versagt,
dem steigt der Aberglauben ins Fenster.
Wer die Engel Gottes verjagt,
den quälen Satans Gespenster!

Aus der greulichen Liste verderbenbringenden Aberglaubens seien einige hauptsächlichsten Erscheinungsformen angeführt:
Zeichendeuterei; Es gibt Zeichen, die Glück oder Unglück bringen sollen, . . .
Auf Zahlen achten: Wenn man bestimmte Zahlen als Glücks—oder Unglücks Zahlen ansieht . . .
Tagewählen: Auf gewisse Tage, Stunden, Zeiten achten beim Tun oder lassen . . .
VOGELschrei beachten: wenn das Käuzchen lockt . . .
Beschwörungen: um Glück zu rufen, Unglück abzuwehren . . .
Sterndeuterei; astrologischen Kalender benutzen zum säen, pflanzen, . . .

Zauberei: während die "Weisze Magie" gewöhnlich unter
einem "natürlichen" . . .
Wahrsagerei: Vergangenheit erforschen, Zukunft deuten . . .
Astrologie: Sterndeutekunst, eins der gröszten Verblen-
dungsmittel Satans . . .
Besprechen: von Krankheiten bei Menschen und Vieh
durch . . .
Pendeln: um Krankheiten und deren Heilmittel festzu-
stellen, . . .
Moderne Heilmethoden: Telepathie, Hypnose, AKU-
PUNKTUR, YOGA, . . .
Schwarze Magie: Das "6 and 7 Buch Mose," ein gefährliches
altindisches Zauberbuch, hat mit der Bibel nichts zu tun, . . .
Modernen Theologie: Ist oftmals eine dämonische irreführung
im Spiel . . .
Zaubersegen: Formel-Gebete, Segen zum Blutstillen, . . .
Ungehorsam gegen Gottes Wort und Willen, ist eine Zauberei-
sünde . . .
Irrlehren heidnischen, philosophischen Aberglaubens . . .

  This is followed by two pages of admonitions, warnings
and directions to the *einen Weg zur völligen Freiheit.*
  The list of objectionable practices brings back memories
of my paternal grandmother. She would concur. The list may
seem all inclusive. My grandmother would have added yet
another item. As a Mennonite I was taught it is wrong to swear
(take an oath). A firm yea or nay are all that is allowed by the
Bible and should be sufficient. Consequently *gewisz* and *sicher*
were stricken from my German vocabulary lest I inadvertently
use them and be consigned to the everlasting fire for all
eternity.
  The last line on the pamphlet says, *"Wirf dieses Blatt
nicht weg, sondern gib es jemand, dem es zum Segenwerden
Kann."* Mr. Schmidt thrilled me by giving it to me. I have no
intention of passing it on, and if any of you want to read it in

its entirety, you will have to come to Freeman. I do not
consider this an undue hardship.

When it came time to leave the Schmidts, the irreverent
Mennonite with the sidelong glances was a crosseyed Mennonite. How about any irreconcilable differences? I think Mr.
Schmidt answered that every time he introduced me to one of
his friends on the steps of that old Evangelical Lutheran
church in Crespo. The answer made me glow with a feeling of
fellowship. He ended each introduction with a trace of pleasure in his voice as he said, "*Und Ihre Sitte sein gerad wie
Unsere.*"

Journal editor's note: There is some discrepancy as to the origin of
this song. As Emma Haynes noted to Ruth Amen in her letter of
April 1, 1973:

> In the booklet "Folklore of the Germans from
> Russia" which was distributed at the Lincoln Convention,
> the words of the "Immigration Song" which was sung by
> three Mennonite women are given. The accompanying notes
> say that this song was composed on July 30, 1874, by Jakob
> Stucky. I was inclined to question this right away because
> I had previously seen reference to the song in connection
> with emigration from Germany to America in 1848. Last
> week I asked the director of the German Folksong Archive
> in Freiburg, Germany, if he could tell me the background,
> and I sent him a Xerox copy of the two pages from the
> Lincoln booklet. He answered by sending me a Xerox copy of
> the same song and said that it was composed in 1845 by a
> man named Samuel Friedrich Sautter and was published
> that same year in Karlsruhe.
>
> Evidently Elder Stucky disapproved of the original
> verses which mention:

> *Und als wir an das Ufer traten*
> *Kehr'n wir in eine Wirtschaft ein.*
> *Wir trinken eine gut' Flasch Wein*

Und lassen Heimat, Heimat sein.

Instead, he substituted such lines as "*Wir fürchten keinen Wasserfall, Der liebe Gott is überall.*"

Dr. Brednich, the director of the archives, was fascinated by these changes and has added the Lincoln notes to the original song. But it really isn't technically correct to say that it was composed by Stucky.

Ye Olde Morality: Frontier Courtship, Dakota Style

This paper was given at the Freeman Centennial Celebration, July 1979.

The grandparents of those of you my age and older didn't talk about space shuttles, or television, or microwave ovens. If we would have mentioned microchips they would probably have told us to throw them on the fire with cow chips. These words were not a part of their vocabulary. This is not surprising.

What did startle me was to learn that they didn't associate love with marriage either. The song "Love and Marriage go together like a horse and carriage" was written long after the horse and buggy days of grandpa and grandma. Love was not reason enough to get married in their day.

The propositions that love makes the world go round, or that all the world loves a lover were probably invented by the same man that conned some of us into believing for a short while that two can live as cheaply as one . . . long after grandpa and grandma were married.

There is much evidence that grandpa and grandma did not get married because they loved one another.

But before we start feeling sorry for grandpa and grandma, we must remember that they are the ones that first talked about "The Good Old Days" and mourned their passing. To see what the Good Old Days were really like in the field of matrimony, let's go back to New Year's Day in 1859 and see what the first legal marriage in Dakota was like.

The first marriage in Dakota Territory conducted according to the legal forms then recognized occurred on the

1st day of January, 1859, at the house of Louis St. Onge, on
Big Sioux Point in Union County, according to an early issue
of the *Yankton Press & Dakotian*.

The groom was John Claude, and the bride was a dusky
maid of the forest and a relative of the St. Onge family. The
ceremony was performed by John H. Charles, then a Justice of
the Peace of Sioux City. He was assisted in the ceremony by
Enos Stutsman, Yankton pioneer, who "made a prayer, sang a
song and delivered a lecture to the newly wedded couple
which, coming from a bachelor, contained some astounding
statements and advice in which he did not appear to consider
the physical endurance of the groom."

"After the ceremony, dancing commenced to the squeaky
music of a cheap fiddle in the hands of a negro named John
Brazeau, who lived with the Indians, and whose boast it was
that he was, 'De fust white man who built a house in Dakota
Territory.' At a late hour the festivities ceased, and the party
adjourned to a neighboring cabin where a feast had been
prepared. The appetite of the guests was sharpened by the
vigorous exercise of swinging a 200 pound squaw through the
rapid and muscular changes of a Big Sioux cotillion, and all
partook most heartily of the viands set before them, and it was
not until after their hunger was fully appeased, and they took
time to examine the appearance of the remnants before them,
that the truth fastened upon their minds that dog meat was
not at all unsavory."

Although this was the first marriage in the Territory
under a quasi-legal ceremony, it did not prove a happy or
enduring one. At the end of two weeks the bride deserted her
husband and returned to the parental tepee, alleging as an
excuse for her action the astounding assertion that she could
not sleep with her husband because his feet gave forth an odor
directly the opposite of the exhalations of the night blooming
cereus.

So much for the proposition that they "Lived happily ever
after."

With the exception of the menu, not much has changed in the wedding celebration, but the path to the altar has been altered greatly.

What did a young couple have to do one hundred years ago to arrive at this happy state of affairs? Actually they had to do very little, it was all done for them.

Marriage was too important to be entrusted to youth, love, or passion. Indeed, matrimony was the royal road to wealth and social advancement. So the essentials were left to the parents, not to such unimportant people as the potential bride and bridegroom.

Before the turn of the century an arranged marriage was universally accepted. It was approved by a wide array of cultures and ethnic groups. It was approved by almost all—except some of the young people involved. We know of some instances where some young people did not relinquish their single status cheerfully. They did not like to have their marriages contracted for propriety, propagation, and property rights. But the time honored tradition of the arranged marriage had all the persuasive powers of a fully loaded shotgun pointed at the head of a reluctant groom by the irate father of the weeping bride. Not much has been said about the bleak, unhappy marriages that resulted.

Much more exposure has been given to those who were too cheerfully romantic without the proper blessings of matrimony. Grandmothers that couldn't read or write could count to nine backwards.

Unlike the 1859 wedding, these arranged unions were binding. Divorce was unheard of in spite of the absence of romantic love and an inattention to personal hygiene.

The seemingly casual approach to such an important event can best be illustrated by a case history in my home community.

Herr and Frau Graber decided by whatever methods parents arrived at such decisions that their son Jakob was ready for matrimony. Once this decision was made, there remained the question of "Who?" After carefully weighing the matters of social and economic status within the community, it was decided that the daughter of Rev. Christian Mueller would be a logical choice. With this problem resolved the *Stökelmann* (Marriage Broker) was summoned.

As he was wont to do, the Stökelmann readily agreed but surprisingly he had a request. Normally the Stökelmann guarded the privacy of his work jealously, but in this instance he asked for permission to take a friend along.

Since the Stökelmann lived in Freeman and Rev. Mueller lived on the other side of the community—almost in the Hurley area— the ride out and back would be long and lonely. Would the Grabers mind if he took a friend along to while away the hours? The Grabers were reasonable people and readily agreed.

The next morning the Stökelmann and his crony set out for the Mueller homestead with horse and buggy. The early morning hours held forth the promise of an extremely hot day. The sun slipped up over the horizon like a searing orb in a cloudless sky. Bird songs were stifled in parched throats by the oppressive heat. The dust raised by the horse's hooves and the buggy wheels hung thick and motionless in choking clouds. The two couriers in the buggy agreed, it was going to be a hot day indeed.

Even at a slow walk it was unlikely that the horses would be able to endure the trip to the Muellers and back. At this slow pace they would only be by Joe Waltner's by noon. When they should be turning back to Freeman they were only a little over half way to their destination. Well—they would stop by Waltner's at noon, water and rest the horses, join the Waltners for dinner, and then decide whether to go on or return to Freeman.

Suddenly the Stökelmann was jolted from his lethargy by the pangs of a new and wonderous idea. It was a stroke of genius! Not only did Joseph Waltner have one—he had three daughters of marriageable age. Not only were these daughters blessed with good health, they were large and strong and able to work hard and long. Their piety could be taken for granted for theirs was a religious family. Joseph Waltner was the song leader in the congregation which ranked him only slightly below the deacons and the minister. The only imaginable blemish in this revised plan would be an objection by Herr and Frau Graber. But surely they too must realize what a hot day this is.

Joe Waltner received his unexpected guests graciously. He helped water and feed the horses while Mrs. Waltner and the three girls set extra plates at the table. The Waltners commiserated with their guests as they told of the difficulties imposed on their mission by the unprecedented heat. They commended the Stökelmann most heartily on his wisdom and ingenuity when he told them of his latest inspiration.

Thus encouraged, the hot travelers aborted their trip to the Muellers and returned to Freeman. The Grabers were indeed reasonable people and commended the Stökelmann on his creative thinking. And thus it came to pass that a gentleman, who for many years held one of the highest elective offices in Hutchinson County, had a Waltner instead of a Mueller for a mother.

To be the beneficiary of this age-old tradition you had to have a family to look after your welfare—to do the arranging. A substantial number of young men, forsaking parents and fatherland, came to the Dakotas alone. Bereft of parental intercessors, it would seem they were consigned to a life of celibacy. Enter a most unlikely benefactor—the local editor. The February 19, 1880, issue of the *Marion Gazette* carried the following article, not as a paid advertisement but as a public service.

"Letter to the marriageable young ladies of Turner County: This being leap year, and as the young men of this town are noted for their native modesty, taken in connection with the fact that nearly, if not quite all, are newcomers, and perhaps have not had the opportunities to become acquainted with you, we say, that in view of the facts as above stated, we deem it our duty to present to your notice the names of the young men in Marion and vicinity who are now in the matrimonial market. They are as follows . . . ." The editor listed thirty-six names.

The editor was dumbfounded when brickbats instead of accolades were the indignant response from his would-be beneficiaries. Before physical violence could render our misguided cupid insensible, an unknown lady got him off the hook with a letter of reply. In the March 11 issue of the *Gazette* the editor could gloat . . .

". . . A short time ago we published a list of marriageable young men in town. Some of the boys were mad enough to eat two eggs, but they won't be mad any more when we tell them that last week one of the young men whose name was published in that list, received a letter written in a dainty feminine hand which reads about in this wise: 'You will pardon the liberty I take in addressing you, but I saw your name in a list of marriageable young men, published in the *Marion Gazette* (sent me by a friend) a few days ago, and as this is leap year, I claim the privilege of a correspondence. I am considered good looking, am moral, and respectably connected. If you deign to answer this, I will in my next give to you my true name and address.' "

Unfortunately a fire destroyed the *Marion Gazette* and all the files shortly after this article appeared. We do not know the ultimate outcome of the above incident. But the winds that whipped the flames that consumed the *Marion Gazette* also wafted a hint of changes to come to wary parents and whispered the hope of better ways to the young.

Surprisingly it was the girls that initiated the changes. I don't know for sure but I would assume that at this time the phrase "the predatory female" was coined. Instead of relying on the parents, piety, and productive work to get a mate they would resort to subterfuge if need be. They would make themselves attractive by any expedient method. To do this they knew they would have to change their image. One of the first citadels of conservative symbolism to fall among my people was the basic black, unadorned clothing.

No longer were the girls content to appear fat, frugal, and fertile. They now strove mightily to appear attractive, available, and amorous in searching for the most exciting combination of guile and dress. They started experimenting with their clothing, an instinct Eve had demonstrated eons ago when she seductively manipulated a fig leaf.

Not only did they lose weight, they shunned even the appearance of weight. The bustle went. There would be no more snide remarks about that thing—that "Deceitful Seat Full."

It seemed the time had come for truth in advertising . . . well at least some truth. True the bustle was discarded but now other unseen unmentionables, harder to detect than the bustle, started to shape the body. The boys weren't fooled—but they didn't mind.

"A citizen of Bon Homme, weight about 250 pounds, unmarried, recently divested a young lady of a set of corsets during a thunder storm because she was afraid the steel in them would attract the lightning. Barney says it was an attractive business all around" (*Yankton Press & Dakotian,* June 9, 1876).

Caution was thrown to the wind and hemlines began to creep up, and shamelessly exposed dainty ankles ensconsed in high, buttoned shoes. Arms were bared. Heavy materials in dark colors gave way to white translucent materials woven of the gossamer fabric of angel hair. All were designed to stimulate the libido of the most lethargic male. Chortled one, whose will to resist had eroded considerably:

"If I suppress a wish for sinful action
My heart glows with inner satisfaction.
But if I'm unsuccessful in restraining
The beast in me—it's also very entertaining."

He must have expressed the sentiment of many. Unscrupulous tabloids began to publish pornographic pictures. The pin-up girl was born. Not all approved. One old codger in my church published a book in which he grumped: "With the better conditions came the tendency to preen oneself. Nice and simple is a virtue, but this is not always uppermost in the minds of the vain. Stiff collars and cuffs, neckties, watch chains, and frequently by the ladies' frilly clothes, hats adorned with feathers or flowers and the like seemed a necessity which led to all manner of strife and disunion. Be not conformed to this world, and, That women adorn themselves in modest apparel, with shamefacedness and sobriety, were appropriate scriptures on which these precepts were founded" (P. R. Kaufman).

The press in South Dakota was divided on the issue. The editors of the *Gregory Times* and the *Woonsocket News* exchanged barbs.

"A few years ago when women began to wear shorter skirts, fashion decreed that a lovely ankle was necessary. A little later a shapely calf was the desire of most women, while today it is a well rounded knee. What will be next?"

To which the young man on the *Woonsocket News* replies:

"You are a young man, Warner; Just be patient. Sit still. Don't rock the boat. Think of the blind man!"

Countered yet another editor: "Cut it out and leave the poor girls alone. Of all the foolish rot that is being sent to the Knocks and Boosts column, this everlasting criticism surely is the limit. What is to you, all you wise guys and geniuses, what the girls wear or don't wear? Clothes don't make the girl any more than they make the man.

"Come here to Hancock and see our real red-blooded American girls romping around with knickers and overalls on, jumping into a grain tank or a flivver, driving out into the country to see the threshers or take a dip in the lake, plumpful of life and good-heartedness and a little mischief, maybe, but

I'll bet you a hole in a doughnut that there isn't an evil thought in their bobbed heads, bless their little hearts."

We could go on and on talking about the ladies—men often do, you know—but what about the men?

While the girls were busy changing their image with clothes, the boys were not just standing idly by as interested spectators. They were spending time and money on the mating game also, but not on clothing.

When the first cars appeared the boys were absolutely enthralled. There developed a dilemna, a conflict of interest. They loved girls but they also loved the horseless carriage. They would work out something!

The Huggy Buggy Ride was doomed. The romance of the surrey with the fringe on top and the one-horse open sleigh were consigned to memory's attic and sentimental movies. "In My Merry Oldsmobile" led the hit parade of top tunes.

When the first cars appeared they were the exclusive domain of macho males. Then they were a status symbol for

The young took over the family flivver with a vengeance.

the wealthier families. And soon they were comandeered by the young.

The young took over the family fliver with a vengeance. In one fell swoop old courting traditions were doomed. With the car came mobility, with mobility came freedom, and with freedom came worry for parents. Parents didn't know where their offspring were and haven't known their whereabouts to this day.

In the good old days a father's concern was divided between his offspring and his buggy and horses.

When another new innovation, flash photography, revealed that some of their sons were actually letting young ladies sit behind the wheel and drive the car, fathers became totally concerned about the car.

Mother also was concerned, but unlike the father, she did not worry herself about someone else's son or car—she worried about her daughter.

I have it on good authority that a certain girl asked her mother for permission to go to a party in the neighborhood. The mother gave a flat "No!" The daughter asked, "Why not?"

Replied the mother, "I've heard what goes on at the parties now days. Some young man is bound to turn up with his father's car. He will ask you if you want some lemonade. You will say, 'I don't mind.' Then he will ask if you would like to go for a ride in his father's car and you will say, 'I don't mind.' Then he will drive to some secluded spot and ask if he may stop the car and you will say, 'I don't mind.' Then he will put his arms around you—and that's when I start worrying!"

Then as now, the daughter eventually had her way and went to the party. As the night wore on the mother spent sleepless time in bed, tossing about, wide awake. Finally, in the wee hours of the morning she heard the chug, chug, chug of a car coming up the driveway. She heard a car door slam and the clatter of footsteps running to the house. The house door opened and closed and her daughter dashed to the mother's bedside. Breathlessly, she exclaimed, "Oh mother it was just wonderful. It was exactly like you said it would be. You would have been so proud of me. Johnny was there with his father's car. He asked me if I would like some lemonade and I said, 'I don't mind.' He then asked me if I would like to go for a ride and I said, 'I don't mind.' We drove to a secluded spot and asked if we should stop and I said, 'I don't mind.' And then, mother, you would have been so proud of me! Before he could put his arms around me, I put my arms around him, and told him, 'Now, let *your* mama do the worrying!' "

Girls in fast cars were considered fast girls. Parents continued to worry. Fathers worried when the car was moving, mothers worried when the car stopped.

Fathers had visions of the family car in the ditch. There would be cries of "get a horse" or "I told you so."

Fathers had visions of the car being totaled in a wreck. These things were known to occur. You could read about it in the papers.

Percentagewise, Kansas City, Missouri, had an unsurpassable automobile accident record in 1899. There were only two cars in the city at that time, and they collided in the main street.

These things didn't only happen in far-off places like Kansas City. They happened right here in South Dakota. And they got you nothing but bad publicity.

The Centerville paper reported the following: "The blue devil-wagon that Doc Sid Headly brought back from Michigan made a record last Sunday evening and nearly butted the pearly gates off their hinges for some of the local boys.

"It seems that on the way back from the ball game in Irene they made a mile in a minute and three quarters and were going for better time when the machine rolled. One man was bruised up.

"The car wasn't damaged too badly. It was righted up and a tire which was busted was filled with oats and the journey resumed. The boys lost their hankering for a mile a minute speed. It is very dangerous and unlawful to run at greater speed than twenty miles per hour and the practice should be frowned upon."

But then the hazards of the automobile were so great that a man could get hurt by the car even if it was standing still. Not only girls were in jeopardy when the car was motionless.

"Gust Schultz had an accident while trying to look into the radiator with a match to see how the water was. He had wood alcohol in the radiator and an explosion was the result. One eye and one ear were badly burned. We mention this as a warning."

The greatest pressure the boys felt was the need to have a superior car. The flashier the car the smoother your royal road to romance. But if an inferior car was devastating, can you imagine what it must have been like to have no car? A Yankee horse trader was considered the sharpest huckster to invade the Dakota prairie. He was a novice compared to a determined South Dakota boy, without a car. These South Dakota lads invented the slogan "All's fair in love and war."

Two car-less Freeman boys developed a ploy that is a marvel of ingenuity. They assembled a vehicle, photographed it and sent pictures to girls at a distance—girls so far removed that they wouldn't know these boys didn't really have a car.

Girls that didn't know the simple expedient of removing the shafts from a carriage didn't automatically qualify it as a horseless carriage.

Girls that didn't know that a couple of empty syrup cans wedged between the spring leaves had nothing to do with illumination.

Girls that didn't know that a sprocket wheel borrowed from a piece of machinery couldn't steer this contraption.

Girls that wouldn't notice there was no motor or drive chain.

Charles Unruh found just such a girl in North Dakota and they are still living together in North Dakota.

So much for "all's fair in love and war"—how about "all the world loves a lover?" The *Yankton Press and Dakotan*, July 2, 1924, reported that automobile speeding, parking conditions, and an anti-petting ordinance were discussed at the city commission's regular meeting—with no action taken. The Yankton city commission was all heart.

On the state level, the attorney general too showed some laws had heart instead of teeth.

To those who are in financial embarrassment and matrimonially inclined it will be glad news that the attorney general ruled that county judges have no authority to accept fees for performing marriage ceremonies.

But how about that man that owned the desolate piece of property that the young cherished as lover's lane? How did he respond to all that traffic?

"Shut the gate lover boy, your heifer is much easier to catch than mine." Now he had heart. He didn't say, "Absolutely no trespassing," all he asked was that they shut the gate.

So we can pat each other on the back and hug our spouses and proclaim that in our lifetime we have reached that place where people now marry only for love. I submit as evidence my latest clipping: this ad that was received by the *Brandon Valley Reporter* in August of 1982.

"Single 45 year old farmer wants to meet 30 year old woman with a tractor. Object marriage. Please send a picture of the tractor to Route 1, General Delivery, Brandon."

At least this marriage doesn't have the urgency some of our modern marriages have. "The farmer plans to answer all replies but it may not be till closer to spring. He won't need the tractor till after the spring thaw."

So how did you and I get here? Are we as we would like to think, the love child of a long line of romantic idealists, or are we a product of genetic engineering manipulated by stern ancestors?

More important—what concepts are we passing on to future generations? I like the way Erich Segal, the man who wrote *Love Story*, articulates it. It is a concept I would like my grandchildren to have.

"The one worthy idea to pass on to future generations is—that for each, his own special woman is unique in the universe. That modern lovers of both sexes, feel that the object of their attraction is the 'One and only.' "

Love is something that all of us reinvent—every time that special feeling strikes us. So just to make things clear, I invented love—the day I set eyes on the lady who is now my wife.

The Mountains Are My Sanctuary

This account of the Anabaptist movement was pre-sented at the Hutterthal Mennonite Church, Freeman, South Dakota, in a series of lectures in the early 1980s.

Die Berge sind mein Gottes Haus,	"The mountains are my sanctuary
Der Yodel mein gebet.	The Yodel is my prayer.
Dort droben auf den Bergen	High upon the mountain tops,
Der Herr Gott selber steht.	The Lord himself is there."

It was in the shadows of these three mountains, the Jungfrau, Mönch, and Eiger, in Berne Canton, in Switzerland, that the faith of my fathers, the Mennonites, the Hutterites, and the Amish, collectively known as the Anabaptists (adult or believer's baptism), had it origin.

It was around New Year's Day in 1519 that Ulrich Zwingli came up the Limat River by boat and stepped ashore by the Wasserkirche in Zurich. The thirty-five-year-old priest had just returned from Rome where he had served as chaplain to the Pope's Swiss Guards. He had come to take charge of Zurich's main cathedral, the Grossmunster.

The Anabaptist movement was spawned in the wake of the turbulence created by Martin Luther in neighboring Germany. Martin Luther spent his entire life teaching and preaching at the University of Wittenberg. His priestly duties included marching illiterate German ploughboys around this church in Wittenberg teaching them the virtue of chastity with these studies.

He explained that while they presented an enticing appearance of virtue and belief, they kept hidden a vile and corrupt persona. Those of you who were in the army during

World War II will remember this ploy was used by the medical corp to caution lusty young soldiers with posters of wholesome looking girls and the legend, "She may look clean, but . . . ."

It was to the door of this church that Martin Luther nailed his Ninety-five Theses in 1517. With this gesture, Luther did not appeal to his illiterate ploughboys with symbolic figures and the German language. It was not his intent to incite the people; he wanted to reform his church and addressed his grievance to the clerics and scholars in Latin.

The year 1517 was the twenty-fifth anniversary of the discovery of America by Columbus. It was only two years after Magellan sailed around the world. It would be another two years before Ulrich Zwingli would become involved in our story. The Hutterites, Mennonites, and Amish are offshoots of the Zwingli branch of the Reformation.

The Swiss Reformation was set in motion by Zwingli, at Zurich. Zwingli, like Luther, successfully challenged the doctrine of indulgences and the attempt to sell them.

Like Luther, he attacked abuses, and made the Scriptures the criterion of truth. Both men preached directly from the Bible.

But Zwingli's interpretations of Scripture were not identical with those of Luther.

On the question of the Eucharist the two held fundamentally divergent views. Luther, rejecting the Roman doctrine of transubstantiation, substituted for it the doctrine of consubstantiation, affirming the real presence, though in another form.

Zwingli denied the real presence altogether, claiming that the Lord's Supper was purely commemorative. This is the position held by Mennonites and Hutterites to this day.

Zwingli was quite tolerant, willing to recognize as legitimate much wider diversities of opinion than Luther, who denounced Zwingli almost as energetically as he denounced the Pope.

In the main, Lutheran Protestantism predominated in north Germany and the Scandanavian countries, Zwingli's non-Lutheran Protestantism spread from Switzerland to France, the Netherlands, and Scotland. Anabaptists, in much smaller numbers, took their message to Germany, the Netherlands and eastern Europe.

The rise of Zurich Anabaptism occasioned the birth of the first known "free church" to arise from a Reformation setting—also the point of departure for the Hutterian movement.

In 1520 Zwingli lost his papal pension as chaplain. That same year Luther burned the Papal Bull and was excommunicated (Wittenberg).

Three major events took place in Zwingli's life in 1523. (1) Luther had debated the Pope's emissaries at Worms and was protected by his friends. Hus had debated the Pope's emissaries at Constance and was burned at the stake. Now the

George Blaurock left the Catholic Church to become an Anabaptist missionary.

Conrad Grebel, leader of the Anabaptist movement.

Bishop of Constance came to Zurich to debate Zwingli. The Zurich city council saved Zwingli's life. (2) Some of Zwingli's disciples start agitating for a believer's church which could only be joined by a public confession of faith, sealed with adult baptism. (3) Blaurock came to Zwingli for counseling.

George Blaurock was a priest from Chur in eastern Switzerland. His name wasn't really Blaurock, but he was called that because he always wore a blue coat. He was also known as "Strong George." He was strong and impulsive, much like the apostle Peter. He left the Catholic Church in 1523 and came to see Zwingli for help in resolving his religious doubts. Zwingli's answers were unsatisfactory and he cast his lot with Grebel's radicals. That move made him the link with the Reformation and the Hutterites.

Conrad Grebel is considered the foremost leader in the Anabaptist movement. Grebel was born into one of Zurich's leading families. For two generations before Conrad, Grebels

Felix Manz, a former Catholic priest, died an Anabaptist martyr.

had been very influential, not only in Zurich but in all of Switzerland. Conrad's father, Jacob, served as a representative of Zurich in practically all of the meetings of the Swiss Confederacy, as well as serving frequently as plenipotentiary in important Swiss and foreign negotiations.

For a time the Grebel family lived across the street from the mayor of Zurich.

At another time the elder Grebel was the bailif or ruler of the district of Grunigen, east of Zurich, and then the Grebels lived in a medieval castle.

Conrad Grebel had close relatives among the noble families living in other castles in the surrounding territory. Some of them were related to the Imperial family of the Hapsburgs who had come from west Zurich. In fact, Conrad's brother was a courtier in their Vienna court. Conrad had studied at universities in Vienna and Paris. During that time he led a rather irregular life, enjoying his family's wealth and

Menno Simons, the former Catholic priest who became a leader of the Mennonites.

position. Some think his excesses at that time caused his early death. He died in prison one year after he launched the Anabaptist movement by performing the first adult baptism. His premature death surely saved him from a martyr's execution.

Felix Manz was the illegitimate child of a Catholic priest. Manz's father was for a time the head of the clerical institutions in the city, with their land holdings. He was a priest with a doctor's degree in theology. In accordance with the corrupt practices of the time, priests were forbidden to marry, but they nevertheless lived in adultery or in common law marriages. He had several children of whom Felix was one.

Zwingli's house stands behind the Grossmunster Cathedral. Neustadtgasse (New-town Street) leads to the east. Here lived Felix Manz with his mother. The exact apartment is not known. The priests openly acknowledged their children at that time, so even if Felix was an illegitimate child, he enjoyed all the privileges which his father's rank brought him, especially a classical education.

In 1524, in the northern Netherlands, Menno Simons was ordained as a priest in the Catholic Church, a position he would hold for eleven years before he would renounce his church and the priesthood. He would eventually accept the mantel of leadership of a severely persecuted group of non-Lutheran Protestants. It was his name that would eventually be given to the Mennonites.

That Menno Simons founded the Mennonites is absolute fiction. The group he would nurture didn't even exist when he became a priest. Menno Simons didn't renounce the priesthood and the Catholic Church till 1535. The Anabaptist movement spawned the Swiss Brethren (as they called themselves) in 1525.

The year 1525 was a momentous year. Martin Luther married Catherine von Bora, who had been a nun, and on Easter Sunday, Zwingli and the Zurich City Council abolished the mass, removed statues and relics from the Grossmunster, and the Reformed Church was born. Easter Sunday, 1525, is the birthday of the Reformed Church, but it was not the first new church to come out of Zwingli's reformation. That distinction had already gone to Conrad Grebel and his Swiss Brethren three months earlier.

On January 17, 1525, the Zurich city council laid down the gauntlet to Grebel and his group. Grebel's insistence on believer's baptism (adult baptism) and separation of church and state had widespread appeal. More and more people no longer brought in their babies for baptism. The city council decided to settle the issue by summoning all those who had offended on this matter to a public debate on Thursday, January 17, 1525. As might be expected, the decision was rendered against the proponents of adult baptism. The next day an order was issued that special meetings for Bible study must be discontinued at once and all unbaptized children must be brought in for baptism within a week.

Four days later, on Saturday night, fourteen members of the Grebel circle met in Felix Manz's home. During the discussion and prayers, George Blaurock became very agitated and begged Grebel to baptize him. Grebel did, and this became the first known adult baptism of the Reformation. Then Blaurock in turn baptized all the other members present. After this they had communion. This Saturday night, January 21, 1525, is recognized by Anabaptists—the Mennonites, the Hutterites, and the Amish—as their anniversary date.

The city council reacted violently. The leaders were thrown in prison and there Grebel died. The outsiders that participated were ordered to leave the city within a week. The council decreed that any others that felt inclined toward adult baptism would die by drowning. Zwingli stalled. He was reluctant to use such harsh measures. The council was insistent.

In prison great pressure was put on Grebel, Manz, and Blaurock to recant and repent. They refused, and Grebel died before he could be tried and executed. On January 5, 1527, almost two years after another January day when Blaurock was baptized in Manz's house, Blaurock and Manz were together again when their sentences were read. Since Blaurock was not a citizen of Zurich he could not legally be executed, so he was sentenced to be flogged and exiled from the city. Manz as a citizen of Zurich would pay the supreme price.

While Blaurock was being led to the city gates for his flogging, Manz was led by the executioner from the prison to the Limat River, close to the spot where Zwingli stepped ashore on yet another January day only six years earlier. In the entourage following Manz to the water were two preachers who admonished him to recant and save his life. If he would do so by three o'clock his life would be spared. His mother and brother were also present and called out words of encouragement and asked him to be steadfast. Felix Manz praised God for this rare opportunity to testify for the truth with his life. He was tied with his hands around his knees and a stick was thrust between his knees and elbows. One account says he was then put in a large sack. When the clock on the tower struck three he called out in a loud voice, "Into thy hands, Father, I commit my spirit." He was forthwith thrust under the water by the executioner and held there with a long pole till, as the execution order demanded, "No more bubbles shall come to the surface."

The day that I stood by the spot stained by the violent death of Felix Manz the waters were tranquil and a swan peacefully preened its white feathers on the dark waters of the Limat. In far-off Holland, Menno Simons was finishing his second year in the priesthood, little knowing what effect this day's happenings would have on his life in another nine years.

Felix Manz's death opened the floodgates of persecution. A *Taufer Kammer* (Anabaptist Commission) was created. They in turn commissioned *Taufer Jaeger* (bounty hunters). They received 250 coins of the realm for every woman they caught, 500 for every man, 1,000 for a deacon, and 2,000 if they brought in a minister. The project was funded by an Anabaptist fund, paid for by the victims. Like our present war on drugs, all people apprehended had all of their property confiscated by the state and the proceeds were put into the Anabaptist Extermination Fund.

During the time of Luther, the Emperor Charles was so preoccupied with political worries, including a series of wars with France on his west and the constant dread of invasion by the Turks on his eastern frontier, that, though a devout Catholic, he had little time to spare for the religious questions then agitating his reign. Protestants, therefore, had a fairly free hand during this period.

During this brief respite from Austria's domineering ways, little Moravia, along with its neighbor Tyrol, allowed Anabaptists to come in and help rebuild their devastated lands. While the Moravian government allowed it, the Moravian church actively encouraged it. The Swiss Brethren flowed into Tyrol and Moravia. There was another reason as well.

Banished from Zurich, Blaurock began his missionary travels through Austria and northern Italy, establishing numerous fellowships on the southern slopes of the Alps. This was Blaurock's field of endeavor. He was very successful. By 1529, only two years after Blaurock was exiled in Zurich, there were 120 known localities in Tyrol with Anabaptists. One source credits him with baptizing 4,000 converts, another gives a more modest 1,000. The best remembered convert was Jacob Hutter, whom we will meet shortly. By now Blaurock's days were numbered.

In 1526, Archduke Ferdinand I of Austria won his big war but was too weakened by it to force his will on the two little countries of Tyrol and Moravia, so the Anabaptists continued to thrive there for a few more years. By 1529 Ferdinand I felt strong enough to subdue Tyrol and put an end to the heretics. By the end of the year, no less than 1,000 had been executed, and the stakes were burning all along the valley of the Inn River. On September 6, 1529, one of those burning stakes consumed the body of our friend, George Blaurock. After being captured, George Blaurock was tried and executed on September 6, 1529.

With Tyrol subjugated, only Moravia remained as a haven for the hapless Anabaptists. How did little Moravia maintain such a high level of independence in the Hapsburg Empire? It was all because of a man then dead for 114 years, John Hus.

East of Austria, in what was Czechoslovakia till this year, is the land of John Hus. Hus was and remains the greatest figure in Czech history and one of the great men of Western civilization. He preached in the Czech language, not in Latin, and compiled the first Czech grammar. Language for him was culture, and culture was the nation. He was burned at the stake as a heretic in 1415. His attachment to language as the cornerstone of national identity and independence was the beginning of a long Czech tradition. It is, perhaps, typical of small, vulnerable populations in general: the mother tongue is the essential home, the one clear barrier between themselves and the stronger, conquering nations. Mother tongue certainly is one of the main ingredients in the glue that holds the Hutterites together. After his death in 1415, 102 years before Luther nailed his Ninety-five Theses to the Wittenberg Cathedral door, his followers organized a Protestant church. They organized an army strong enough to hold Austria at bay. Hus lived in Bohemia. At the southern border was a little country by the name of Moravia. His followers took their Protestantism to Moravia in 1511, ninety-six years after Hus's execution, six years before Luther nailed his Ninety-five Theses to the Wittenberg Church door, and eight years before Zwingli came to Zurich. When Tyrol was totally subjugated by Austria, tiny Moravia with its Protestant army stood alone.

This time is known as the Golden Years in Hutterite history. But even in tolerant Moravia there would be seemingly insurmountable obstacles before this high pinnacle was achieved. And this might be the proper place to discuss the problem and introduce you to Jacob Hutter. This was the incident that separated the Hutterites from the other Anabaptists, incurred the disfavor of some Moravians, and launched the Hutterites on their communal living.

Jacob Hutter, a native of Tyrol, had a scanty education. To earn a living he went to Vienna to learn the hat maker's trade, hence his name, Jacob the hatter/Hutter. He was a natural leader and when Blaurock died he was thrust into his leadership role. He would lead his people for only seven years before he would be captured and burned at the stake. In those seven years, he would put such an imprint on the communal Anabaptists that they would bear his name.

Jacob Hutter's mission was to see if the remnants of the Swiss Brethren in Tyrol could move to Moravia. In the year 1529, Jacob Hutter was sent by his people to visit and counsel with the Brethren in Moravia. He then returned to Tyrol and sent one group after another to Moravia. Most of those that Hutter sent were members of Blaurock's orphaned congregations.

Jacob Hutter and his wife, Katherine, returning to South Tyrol for another group of refugees, were captured. Hutter was tried and executed in Innsbruck on February 25, 1536; his wife was executed two years later.

Katherine's execution was different from that of her husband, Jacob, or Blaurock, or the 1,000 whose burning stakes illuminated the nights along the Inn River in Tyrol in 1529. The preferred method for executing women was by drowning. If the woman was pregnant she was allowed to live until the child was born and placed in an orphanage. Her clothes, with the exception of the undergarments, were removed. Her executioners, like those at Christ's cross, could divide the garments among themselves. Rocks tied to her feet made sure she would sink to the bottom.

The large Anabaptist church of Nikolsburg in Moravia, in contrast to all other Anabaptist groups in the province, approved of military service and differed with them on a few other points. The ruler of the principality of which Nikolsburg was the center, Leonhard von Lichtenstein, was a member of this church. The membership varied from 6,000 to 12,000. Between 200 and 300 dissenting members of the church met separately for worship. Within a short time they were informed by Lichtenstein that they could not remain in Nikolsburg unless they attended the divine services held by the recognized pastors of the congregation. In consequence a company of between 200 and 300 persons departed from Nikolsburg in the spring of 1528. They were not allowed to remove anything from Nikolsburg except such articles as they could carry.

They first camped in a vacated village named Bogenitz. As night fell they chose "Ministers of temporal needs," wrote the chronicler of the Brethren. These men spread a cloak before the people and every one laid down on it his earthly

possessions unconstrained and with a willing mind according
to the teachings of the prophets and the apostles." This was
the beginning of communism by this brotherhood, the organization of the first Bruderhof. Jacob Hutter, whose name this
movement bears, was not present; he wasn't even a member.
He would not meet these people for another year.

This sharing was not an impulsive act improvised on the
spur of the moment. The Anabaptists were and continue to be
biblicists. They believe in strict adherence to the letter of the
Bible. To this day the Hutterites will quickly quote from
memory three Bible passages to justify their communal living
as a divine mandate:

Acts 2:44,45 "And all that believed were together, and
had all things common; and sold their possessions and goods,
and parted them to all men, as every man had need."

Acts 4:32 "And the multitude of them that believed were
of one heart and of one soul: neither said any of them that any
of the things which he possessed was his own; but they had all
things common."

Acts 4:34,35 "Neither was there any among them that
lacked: for as many as were possessors of lands or houses sold
them, and brought the prices of the things that were sold, and
laid them at the apostles' feet: and distribution was made unto
every man according as he had need."

It seems strange that Godless communism would adopt
the same slogan four centuries later, "From each according to
his ability, to each according to his need."

Jacob Hutter, who had led many to tolerant Moravia,
would in one year (1533-35) affiliate with these communitarian Anabaptists and reorganize them through a careful
attention to *Ordnung* (corporate orderliness). From now on
these communitarian Anabaptists would be known as the
Hutterian Brethren, or Hutterites.

After this expulsion from Nikolsburg, the Hutterites
could not find a place to settle down. Like the Children of
Israel, they wandered in the wilderness, sleeping in forests

during the summer and in caves in winter. Once they found a permanent resting place they established many colonies as they grew and prospered. In addition to their skills in agriculture, weaving, building, furniture making, milling, and brewing, they were sought out for their healing arts. French nobility sent their children to be healed and their adults to be treated for "French disease." There are celebrated cases where Hutterite doctors were called to the palaces of nobility where court doctors could not help their sick lords. Some insist Kindergarten is a Hutterite concept. Even if they didn't originate Kindergarten they developed it to such a degree that rulers and magistrates sent their children. Their Habaner pottery was so fine that remaining original pieces are now considered a national treasure, and removal of any of it from the country is strictly prohibited by law. The list goes on.

In this period the brotherhood in Moravia and a few points in Hungary had between forty and fifty colonies with anywhere from 12,000 to 70,000 members.

The Golden Age came to an abrupt end. On November 8, 1620, Frederick's Protestant army was defeated by Catholic forces led by the Duke of Bavaria at the Battle of White Mountain, outside Prague. This was the beginning of the Thirty Years' War. For Frederick and for Bohemia, "the defeat was total," Yates writes. "In Bohemia, mass executions or 'purges' exterminated all resistance. The Bohemian church was totally suppressed and the whole country reduced to misery." Middle Europe was so devastated by this cruel war that it did not recover for a full century—all in the name of Christianity. The Thirty Years' War (1618-1648) pitted Catholics against Protestants, all killing one another for the greater glory of God. Cities were burned down, the armies lived off the land, ruthlessly cutting down men and ravishing the women. The well-filled granaries, sleek cattle, and fine looking horses of the Hutterite colonies offered special temptations to the marauding parties of both armies. Let me illustrate the savage brutality by reading a quote from the *Great Cronik* of the Hutterites.

For 1620—two years after the Thirty Years' War started—the *Great Cronik* records: "One Bruderhof was attacked by 1,500 men. In three hours fifty-two men were killed and another seventeen men and women so mutilated that they died within a few days. For the purpose of wringing from the Brethren a confession of the hiding places of their supposed wealth they burned them with hot irons and flaming torches, poured hot grease over their bare bodies, cut deep wounds into their flesh, which they filled with powder which they then ignited, jerked off their fingers, slashed into them with their swords as though they were cabbage heads. One brother's head they completely twisted about so that he actually faced straight backward."

In September 1662, the Catholics once again gained complete control of the territory and demanded that all Hutterites leave within four weeks or suffer the consequences. In vain the poor people pled that they might at least be given until the next spring to make preparations for leaving, since it was now approaching winter. Their pleadings fell on deaf ears. In the winter they were driven across the border.

In the southeastern corner of what was then Transylvania, or Siebenbergen, but is now Romania, lived a famous prince (Bethlen Gabor). He had been a Protestant general during the war and was favorable to the Protestant sects. He gave the Hutterites a place to live.

Here in Transylvania and Hungary the Hutterites now found a home for another 100 years, but they never recovered the prosperity of their golden years in Moravia. They could not escape the hazards of the wars and invasions that constantly threatened the populations of that troubled part of Europe.

Throughout the latter part of the century their settlements were subjected to continual raids by the Turkish armies that were threatening to overrun all of middle Europe at this time. Frequently in these raids their buildings were burned down, the cattle driven away, the men carried off to the galleys and the women into slavery.

The Austrian army (the Poles say it was the Polish army) finally defeated the Turks at the very gates of Vienna. Would the Hutterites have peace now? Hardly. Maria Theresa, a most devout Catholic, was now the ruler. Like all her Hapsburg predecessors, once the foreign wars were won she set about to bring order in her house by declaring all-out war on the Anabaptists in her realm. To one Delphine, an ardent Jesuit and a confirmed advocate of total extinction, was given the task of either converting the Hutterites to Catholicism or driving them out of the land. He almost succeeded. He came within a hair. A Hutterian Haushaben in Alwinz, Transylvania (Rumania), existed from 1621 to 1767. It was made up of a Hutterite remnant of about forty-eight survivors from the 70,000 former Hutterite membership. The original Hutterian movement of Moravian origin might have collapsed completely had it not been for the unexpected arrival of a group of very unlikely recruits from a totally unexpected quarter.

In the archduchy of Carinthia, a member of the Hapsburg Empire, there appeared just at this time a small band of Lutherans, who, influenced to a large extent by their independent reading of the Bible, and especially of the works of the highly evangelical Lutheran Johan Arndt, an author well known among the Mennonites of the time as well, were more like the Anabaptists in their religious views than the orthodox Lutherans.

Lutherans not being tolerated in Carinthia at this time, Maria Theresa had this small band deported at government expense in 1755 to another of her possessions, Transylvania, where both Catholics and Lutherans were free to exercise their religious views; and where the emigrants were promised new homes and lands upon their arrival. The Lutherans in Transylvania did not meet the requirements of an evangelical New Testament church as the Carinthian brethren had conceived it. Refusing to take the oath of allegiance to the empress which was demanded of them as a pre-requisite to receiving the land grants, they were denied the promised homes. Thus they were set adrift, looking for work and a resting place wherever they could find it. Some of them wandered into Hutterite colonies about Hermanstadt, where they found religious views and practices more like their own than any they had observed. Most of the exiles ultimately joined the colonies and became an integral part of the Hutterite movement from then on. The best evidence perhaps that the Carinthians remained loyal to their choice is the fact that many of the typical names found in the colonies in Dakota and Canada today trace their origin back to these Carinthian Lutherans—Glanzer, Hofer, Klein-sasser, Miller, Waldner. This contingent became the backbone of the Transylvania Hutterite group from this time on, and was perhaps responsible for the restoration of communism among them.

By casting their lot with the despised Hutterites, the new recruits forfeited the toleration promised by Maria Theresa. As Lutherans they would have been tolerated in Transylvania, but not as Hutterites. If they would not be Lutherans they must be Catholics—this they refused to do. So now they shared the common experience of all the Hutterites: their religious practices were forbidden; their leaders were arrested and thrown in prison; and the members of the congregations were scattered by the police throughout various districts so that they could no longer meet together for worship.

Within eight days, forty-six survivors found their way back to Creutz, the last colony destroyed by the Jesuit Delphine. Now the Jesuit Delphine decided to adopt the same deadly measures he had used against the Hutterites when he exterminated them totally in Hungary. The authorities in Hermanstadt (capital of Transylvania) would not allow such brutality without an imperial order, so Delphine went to Vienna to see the empress. While he was gone, the Hutterites, both the new recruits from Carinthia and the faithful remnant of the older group, decided to chance emigration across the

Carpathian Mountains into Wallachia, under Turkish rule, where neither Catholic nor Lutheran nor Hutterite was known. All Christians looked alike to the Turks. By the time of departure, twenty-one more of the scattered brethren had found their way back bringing the total number of escapees to sixty-seven. Others would eventually find the group again in Russia.

In the *Cronik*, Johannes Waldner, who was a participant, recorded the following: "On October 3, 1767, at 10:00 o'clock in the morning, the flight of the congregation took place. The brethren had secured two wagons, one with two pair of oxen and one with the two teams of horses. The brethren and sisters, even the youth of fourteen and fifteen, each took his staff in his hand and a bundle on his back. Many a one carried his infant child on top of his pack. The little children of four and five years had to go on foot. So they departed in the name of God. The well-built houses and much household equipment were left behind unsold.

"So we left Creutz, sixty-seven souls (sixteen of whom were from the old congregation at Alwintz), with heavy hearts at the thought of leaving behind the brethren and sisters who lay in the prison at Herpes and Hermanstadt, but the most of those later succeeded in returning to the brotherhood. No one asked us to halt, for the way was prepared by God."

It must be said that the Hutterites were mightly assisted in their escape by human help also. It was necessary to avoid attracting attention and for this reason a guide was hired who would know every stick and stone of the way and would lead them over the least frequented trails. They would not know if the guide was trustworthy till journey's end.

On the seventh day of the journey, the wagons had to be taken through two villages on the main highway. The guide sent his assistant with the people a roundabout way. He led them to one side of the villages over the mountain and through the valley until they again caught up with the wagons on the highway.

"When we came to the Kronstadt Heath, the guide would neither halt nor rest, but drove on without stop or stay, and our people and wagons did not dare to lag behind for the guide feared that he might be halted. So we hastened that we might pass Kronstadt before daybreak. Hard as the journey by day across Kronstadt Heath was, the night journey was much more trying. That night many a one experienced what had seemed impossible to him before, namely that one can sleep and walk at the same time."

On October 10, the weary group finally reached the high plateau of the Carpathian mountain range which was the last obstacle between them and freedom. Just as they reached the point where they could look into the promised land, a constable discovered them and told them he must go and report them to the authorities.

"At this our anxiety and fear was increased many fold, since we expected nothing else but that we would now all be taken captive." When the constable had gone to make his report another man discovered the group of refugees. He was the escort that was to lead them over their last obstacle. Preparations were made to leave at once, before the constable and his men could return. It was impossible to get over the mountains with the wagons, so the most necessary things were loaded on the four horses. The four oxen were driven across unloaded.

"When everything was ready, just as the sun was setting, we started out again on the thirteenth day of October. The escort took us on untrodden ways through the underbrush and wilderness, where they knew that we were safe and without danger, for they knew all the secret ways and paths of the mountains. At many places we had to climb up on hands and feet. Everyone took care to follow closely so that he would not be left behind. At several places the loaded pack horses were brought up only with great difficulty. So we struggled on during the entire night. Each one can best imagine for himself what a difficult and tedious journey that was . . . with bag and

baggage and little ones on the back. To climb the high mountains with young and old and weak ones . . . and that at night!
The border was at the very top of the mountains."

"The Jesuit Delphine had made arrangements to take our
children from us and put them in an orphanage. This had to be
arranged with the Empress Maria Theresa. Everything had
been prepared in Trenschment outside of Hermanstadt; even
the beds for our children were in readiness. But God had
brought his intentions to naught, and so planned and arranged
that the snare which the enemy laid for us was torn apart, and
when he reached for us we had already fled the land. Praise be
to God, who did not permit us to fall prey to their jaws."

Unfortunately, the arrival of the Hutterites here in what
at first seemed a land of freedom was ill timed. Russia and
Turkey soon engaged in war, and the unlucky victims of so
many troubles found themselves right in the heart of another
battle zone, where the Turks robbed them of property and
money, and sent their men into captivity and galley slavery.
And so, after a few years of those experiences, they decided to
take up the wanderer's staff once more.

When Czar Alexander II revoked the special privileges
his great grandmother Catherine the Great had offered the
Germans to entice them to Russia, the Germans in Russia lost
among other rights their exemption from military service. The
Mennonites and Hutterites sent a delegation to North America
to look for a place to relocate. Of the twelve delegates, two
were Hutterites. The chief Hutterite delegate was Rev. Paul
Tschetter. He directed the Hutterites to South Dakota.

During 1874, the train engine Black Hills No. 1 pulled
the first group of Hutterites, my ancestors, and I imagine some
of yours, to Yankton.

The last of the Hutterites arrived in 1879. The first group
was the Hutterdorf Colony, the communal group. They were
under the leadership of Michael Waldner, a descendant of the
Carinthian Lutherans and a blacksmith. Therefore they and

their descendants are known to this day as *Die Schmeiden Leut,* the Smith people.

They established their colony along the Missouri River west of Yankton, known as Bon Homme Colony.

Another communal group under the leadership of Preacher Darius Walter started Wolf Creek Colony. They are known as the *Darius Leut,* the Darius people.

Elm Spring was the third colony started by the newcomers. Since two teachers were the organizers, people from that colony and its daughter colonies are known as the *Lehrer Leut,* the teacher people.

About 1,300 Hutterites came to Dakota Territory. The vast majority did not elect to live in colonies but homesteaded along the Jim River from south of Olivet to Alexandria, and on the prairies west of Freeman. They joined various Mennonite churches and are known as the *Prairie Leut,* the prairie people.

During World War I, the colony Hutterites were the objects of scorn and hostility and set out in search of refuge in Canada. Again a delegation was sent out. In 1918 twelve colonies moved to Canada, four more were gone by 1934. Only Bon Homme remained in South Dakota. The next year the South Dakota legislature passed a law allowing communal societies to incorporate. The next year, 1935, a colony returned from Canada.

Publishers' note: For additional information about the subject of this talk, please see Victor Peters, *All Things Common: The* *Hutterian Way of Life* (Minneapolis: Univ. of Minnesota Press, 1965).

Princes, Potentates, and Plain People

This paper was presented at the Dakotah Corral of Westerners International in Sioux Falls, South Dakota, spring 1981.

For 460 years Mennonites have deliberately kept a low profile. The lower the better. To be invisible was desirable. To be detected often meant capture and that could mean prison, torture, or even death. They went to extraordinary lengths to remain inconspicuous—this with their Anabaptist beliefs marked them as queer people—they like to think of themselves as plain people. In the 16th, 17th and 18th centuries living conditions for the peasants were primitive and it served the Mennonites well and was quite easy for them to become the "Plain People."

If you think of these people as queer—how about some of those strange fellows that ruled them—the princes and potentates that strutted about the capitals of Europe? Though both parties tried to avoid the other, there were times when their paths crossed—strange princes and potentates, strange people—strange happenings. Yet, in spite of their reticence, there were those occasions when they were confronted by some of the most powerful people in their countries. Though the Mennonites were, and in some quarters still are, considered rather queer, some of their rulers also had some odd peculiarities. It shouldn't seem strange then that when some of these queer plain people and some of those odd autocrats met surprising things happened. If some one else hadn't already coined the title "Plain and Fancy" I would like to use it for this presentation. Since I can't I won't. So let's try, "Princes, Potentates and Plain People."

The idea of talking about "Princes, Potentates and Plain People" was suggested to me by a man that had been dead for 260 years. When I was in school we read a story about this man. He was Peter the Great. When he became Czar of Russia he went to England and Holland to learn their ways. He wanted to learn about western culture and industry so he could teach his backward subjects these things. To get his information he sometimes traveled about those countries *ARTHUR* incognito. When he stopped at a peasant hut for rest and a meal, the housewife had no way of knowing that he was the ruler of one of the world's largest countries. She admitted him into her poor hut and assigned him the task of stirring the soup while she went outside to do some chore. Peter was exceedingly tired and the warmth of the fire soon induced a deep sleep. He didn't stir. The soup boiled over. When the housewife returned she smelled and saw a very scorched kettle. She was just as provoked as a contemporary Mennonite housewife is when the borscht boils over. She grabbed her broom and beat the hapless czar over his head and back. I don't know if this was a Mennonite woman but there were other Mennonites who got involved with other rulers.

Once upon a time, long, long ago, in Poland, there lived a very rich man. No one had ever been this rich in Poland before and no one in Poland has been as rich since. His name was Adam Czartoryski.

He had immense land holdings scattered all over Volhynia and Padolia. His homes were so large and luxurious that they didn't resemble houses but palaces.

When the communists confiscated the estates of the wealthy they converted this place of Adam Czartoryski into the Polish National School of Agriculture.

Though it is now a school, its former splendor is still evident. The vaulted ceilings and the intricate floors and open stairways all speak of great wealth.

In Czartoryski's days, central heating as we know it had not been invented. Ceramic heating stoves stood tall in every

room. When I saw this it occurred to me that something was
amiss. It took me a while to realize there are no doors on the
stove to insert fuel. I asked our guide, "Is this a stove?" She
assured me it was. "How do you put in the fuel?" I asked. She
grinned and explained.

The walls by the stoves are no ordinary walls. There are
two walls with a passageway between. The doors of the stove
open into the passageway. When Adam entertained his fine
friends, he didn't want to offend them with the sight of his
uncouth servants firing the stove. This way he could keep the
ordinary people out of sight while they went about their work.

Since Czartoryski was a man of culture he had an
impressive library. His books were not on display in a large
room in his palace but in an ornate, separate building.

Another imposing building on the palace grounds was a
home he built for one of his daughters. I do not know how
many children Czartoryski had, but we know of at least three.
One was a son, also named Adam, and his second daughter was
married to Duke Leopold Eberhardt of Wurttemberg, who then
ruled, in addition to his lands east of the Rhine, the district of
Montbeliard, south of Alsace, now part of France. When the
elder Adam Czartoryski died, young Adam inherited his
father's vast holdings. The next year he went on a long tour to
inspect his newly acquired estates.

He also went to visit his sister in Wurttemberg, whose
home was the castle on the hill.

Adam noticed the efficiency and simplicity of the girl
servant in his sister's home. He was impressed. He asked his
sister about this girl.

She told him that she belonged to a group of people called
Mennonites with an exceptional farming reputation. Just the
kind of people Czartoryski was trying to get on his lands.

So great was their renown as agricultural experts that
their neighbors wanted to learn their methods. An enter-
prising Mennonite started publishing a popular *Farmers
Almanac* to answer their questions.

But the duchess cautioned her brother that they are also a very peculiar people. All the men wore luxurious beards but would not allow a mustache to grow. No one used buttons, they used hooks and eyes instead. And after communion they washed their feet.

Their churches refused to baptize infants. Only adults are eligible for this sacred rite. They taught against serving in the military.

To this day their churches have no bell towers on the outside and no figures or decorations on the inside.

Since Napoleon appropriated the District of Montbeliard for France the people now speak French, as the scriptures on the wall indicate.

But the old church records in this bookcase are written in German and the descendants of the people that left here still speak German even if they have lived in Russia and America for over two hundred years. People who remain here now speak French.

Stucky and Graber are two common names here and also in Freeman, South Dakota, and in Pretty Prairie and Moundridge, Kansas.

Grabers must be very prolific Mennonites. They are still in abundance in this part of France and wherever else they have settled.

They continue to live and die in the land once ruled by the sister of Adam Czartoryski and her husband, Leopold Eberhardt.

Kaufmans also lived here when Adam Czartoryski visited his sister. It is the Kaufman family story that has passed on to us the story of the girl servant in the home of Adam's sister.

Moses Gerig, whose name would be changed to Moses Gering, is found in the pages of the old records. This ancient ancestor of my wife must have left relatives behind when he left because Gerings still remain, spelling their name in the old fashion.

What does all of this have to do with Adam Czartoryski, his sister, and her Mennonite house servant?

An old document, passed down through the generations, gives us the answer to Adam Czartoryski's final decision about the Mennonite girl and her people.

In spite of their peculiarities, Adam must have been impressed. He induced seven families to leave his sister's service and come to his land in Poland. On this document we see Gerig changed to Gering, but then they also slipped an "n" into Czartoryski's name and spelled it Czartorinski. The passport calls him the prince of Padolia, but he settled these people on some of his land in Volhynia. Ever since the people of East Freeman have been known as the Volhynian Swiss.

The Volhynian Swiss brought two old books with them to Freeman. They were started in a little village named Michelsdorf. Michelsdorf was adjacent to another village named Urszculin. Czartoryski's Polish government made them keep their records in the Polish language. The last Polish entry is dated 1833.

An 1833 marker notes the date of an abortive attempt by the Poles to free themselves from Russian tyranny. Poland had long since ceased to exist. The final partition had obliterated the country in 1795. In 1831 the harassed Poles tried revolution against Russia, and failed. Russia tightened the screws more and the Polish language was abolished.

Now the Mennonites reverted to the use of the German language in their record books. The first entry in German is a boy by the name of Voran, an orphan boy adopted by a Mennonite family.

The next page is a confirmation of the Grabers' continuing prolific ways.

The Mennonites eventually left Michelsdorf and that part of town was incorporated by Urszulin. When some of us visited here several years ago, there was no indication that Michelsdorf and its Mennonite inhabitants had ever existed here. The natives still remember Czartoryski because his palace stands only a few miles from here. Adam spent most of his last thirty years in Paris, trying desperately to induce the French and English to help the Poles evict Russia from Poland.

Another Pole of world renown who also struggled for the Polish cause in Paris was born in this home in 1810, about nineteen years after Czartoryski brought the Volhynian Swiss to Poland. His name was Fredrick Chopin. During the insurrection of 1832, Chopin tried to bolster the morale of the Polish people and wrote his immortal "Etude in C Minor." When the Russian Czar heard it played he exclaimed, "This music is dangerous! It is like guns hidden under beautiful roses." Chopin took refuge in Paris. He composed many beautiful, haunting melodies which were constant reminders of the beauty and suffering of his beloved Poland. Chopin was buried in France. His heart is buried in St. John's Cathedral in Warsaw. The next time you listen to Chopin's music, see if you can't detect in it a mystic beauty, tenderness, and feeling born of the despair felt by Chopin and Czartoryski as they tried to win sympathy and support for their Poland. And also give a fleeting thought to the simple, efficient Mennonite girl in the Duchy of Wurttemberg, whose industry brought the attention of Adam Czartoryski to her people.

I do not know if Maria Theresa or her eldest child, Joseph II, ever personally met a Mennonite or Hutterite. We do know both were aware of and personally involved with both groups. Though Joseph II would eventually rule Austria in his mother's place, the world would better remember his sister, Marie Antionette. She gained her claim to fame by becoming the queen of France and ultimately getting her head lopped off on the guillotine.

When Maria Theresa ascended the throne of Austria, she was threatened by the rulers of several of the countries of Europe, especially Frederick the Great of Prussia. The new empress fled to Hungary and personally appealed to the Hungarian nobles and won their enthusiastic support. When

Joseph succeeded his mother to the throne of Austria, he treated the Hungarians harshly.

When Prussia and Russia conspired to divide Poland, Maria Theresa opposed the plan. Her son Joseph sided with the aggressors and convinced his mother to take a large part of Poland for Austria.

Maria Theresa was a devout Catholic and a most moral person. As the protector of the faith she felt it her duty to exterminate all non-Catholics in the Empire. To her the most offensive heretics were the Hutterites. She appointed a Jesuit by the name of Delphine to exterminate them. He almost succeeded, but a remnant of about forty-five managed to escape and keep that movement alive.

Joseph II in turn invited all manner of Germans to settle those lands he had acquired in the partition of Poland. His invitation was even extended to those brethren of the Hutterites, the Volhynian Swiss. He didn't invite the Hutterites back. Adam Czartoryski had invited those Swiss Mennonites that had found refuge in the Duchy of Wurttemberg. Joseph II extended his invitation to those Swiss Mennonites that had fled to the Palatinate in Germany.

Not only did he invite—he bribed. He offered an equipped farmyard, including a house-barn, shed, and basic implements and equipment. There was to be financial assistance to buy livestock, and limited military exemption.

Because the Mennonites had heard of Marie Theresa's persecution of the Hutterites, they were a bit leery. Before they sold their homes in the Palatinate they approached the Austrian government. On March 20, 1784, the Emperor personally answered their inquiry and assured them of their religious freedom. His mother, Maria Theresa, had been dead only four years. This must have had her spinning in her grave—especially when he sent soldiers to the defense of her despised Mennonites in a caper that might be called "the Cemetery Scandal."

This point of tension developed with the first Mennonite death. An effort to bury him in the local cemetery was resisted by the farmers of the area. They refused to admit the corpse or the funeral procession into the graveyard. The Mennonites appealed to the local government administrators for help. A detachment of the Hungarian Cavalry was sent. They surrounded the cemetery while the Mennonites dug the grave and buried their deceased brother.

Joseph II intervened in person and declared that from now on the cemetery is open to all professing Christians. He said, "My subjects shall live in peace with one another, and their dead shall lie side by side in peace." Rupp Backman was probably the first Mennonite that had a military burial.

Joseph thought it was legend. Another episode of special interest to the Hutterites occurred here seven years after the death of Joseph II. It concerns a man with a very common Hutterite name. It is the story of Andreas Hofer, the national hero of the Tyrol.

Andreas Hofer was an innkeeper, when Napoleon Bonaparte sent a big army into Tyrol to conquer it (1797). The peasants came together and chose Hofer as their leader. Under him they defeated the French and drove them out of the country. Napoleon, however, made a treaty dividing the country between Bavaria and France.

Andreas Hofer would not be subdued so easily. He worked secretly among the peasants, found arms, and told them to be ready to try to win their freedom again. Many of the peasants had no weapons except scythes, pitchforks, and sledge-hammers. One day Andreas Hofer sent a message to all his neighbors: "The time has come." That night he and his friends lit a big bonfire on the Alps above his home to show that they were going to attack their enemies.

Several thousand men gathered around Hofer: he led them over the Alps to Innsbruck, where Jacob Hutter had been burned at the stake. After hard fighting, Hofer's men defeated the powerful Bavarian army. Napoleon, who had conquered almost all of Europe, did not like being defeated by these peasants. He assembled an army of 50,000 men and sent it to Innsbruck. Andreas Hofer fought this great French army and defeated it also. The Tyrolese then elected him governor of their country.

Napoleon made another effort against Hofer, and this time defeated him. Hofer was taken prisoner and shot. He would not allow the soldiers to bind his eyes and he would not kneel, but stood up and cried: "Long live Kaiser Franz! Aim straight!"

Frederick the Great of Prussia and Maria Theresa of Austria started to rule their empires in the same year, 1740. They disliked each other but had similar objectives. Both participated in the partition of Poland. Both tried to induce German farmers to settle on their newly acquired property. Both offered enticing inducements. But in the matter of the Anabaptists they differed markedly. While Maria Theresa tried to exterminate the Hutterites, Frederick the Great invited unpopular sects to his new holdings. Not only Mennonites but Huguenots, Schwenkenfelders, and Salzburgers found asylum in Prussia. Frederick offered the Mennonites full rights of citizenship fifty years before similar privileges were enjoyed by the Mennonites under Polish rule in Danzig. It is said that during his reign (1740-1786) he enlisted no less than 300,000 colonists and established 900 villages and towns. They came in droves without regard for religion or dialect.

It is a small wonder, therefore, that when Poland was partitioned, and the delta region fell to Frederick, the Mennonites were well pleased. In order to express their loyalty to their new king as well as pleasure at his accession, the Low-Germans about Marienburg, on the occasion of a royal celebration, presented him with an appropriate gift from the products of their farms. The list reads like the song "The Twelve Days of Christmas." The grateful Low-Germans gave him two well-

Catherine (II) the Great invited the Mennonites to settle in Russia.

fed oxen ready for the king's table, four hundred pounds of butter, twenty cakes of cheese, together with a large assortment of chickens and ducks.

The king was impressed—he was also in a bind.

Complete religious toleration Frederick had gladly promised, but by this time military exemption had become another matter. He owed too much to a well-organized army in the expansion of Prussia to look with indifference to any shrinking of the supply of available troops. So long as the Mennonite settlements had remained small and scattered, the granting of exemptions did not materially weaken the military strength of the nation. But with the acquisition of the Vistula lowlands he got large, compact areas almost solidly filled with people opposed to the use of military force. Till now Frederick had not been hesitant in providing for the tender conscience of his Mennonite subjects. Now he hesitated.

Frederick finally decided that money was just as essential to the program of conquest as soldiers, and just as hard to get. Since the Mennonites did not draw a fine distinction between direct and indirect service, a compromise was worked out. In return for an annual 5,000 thaler contribution to the Military Academy at Culm, the Mennonites would have complete religious liberty.

Does this name mean anything to you? If I told you her nickname was "Fike," or "Figchen," would you recognize this princess? Even if she was a princess, she was poverty-stricken. She went to Russia but she only had three dresses to her name. She was friendless and penniless.

She managed to marry her third cousin, the Grand Duke Peter, heir to the throne of Russia. She joined the Russian Orthodox Church and changed her name to Catherine. It wasn't a happy marriage. Peter was an imbecile whose pleasures in life were playing with wax dolls dressed in military uniforms and drinking.

Catherine had much time alone. She spent much of it riding about on her favorite horses and seducing her many lovers.

Catherine had several children but her husband refused to claim any of them. Her first child was Paul. She didn't get to raise him either. Queen Elizabeth was still on the throne and wanted to raise him in her own image. Catherine was seldom allowed to see her own children. Her husband hated her and she loathed him. He threatened to divorce her and shut her up in a convent for life. So she staged a revolt and when he became czar she kicked him off the throne.

One of her lovers was Gregory Orlov. He had three powerful brothers and an influential father. Gregory put arsenic in Catherine's husband's vodka. Peter was so ornery he refused to die. So Orlov knocked him down and choked him to death. I read he did this by stuffing a napkin down his throat. My guide in Russia said, "No! no! it was a stocking."

Catherine wore the uniform of Orlov's regiment and with that support gained the crown of Russia. She ruled for thirty-four years after that. She never married again: but she wasn't exactly lonesome. For scores, yea, perhaps hundreds of different lovers, danced in the ballroom of her warm and romantic heart. Yet she was so strict with her grandchildren that she made them stop studying botany because they asked questions about the reproduction of plants. She supported her lovers in regal splendor and squandered $500,000,000 on them.

Potemkin, Catherine II's favorite and most durable lover.

Her favorite and most durable lover was an ugly giant named Potemkin. One of his eyes was glass; he lost the real eye in a barroom brawl. Although Potemkin lived in a palace glittering with all the splendor and riches of Asia, he went about with nothing but house slippers on his bare feet. He never combed his hair (except when a picture was taken) and he always needed a bath. He chewed his fingernails and ate raw onions and garlic. But he was a tornado of physical energy, and the mere touch of his hand filled Catherine with a vast and tender happiness. She called him her "golden pheasant," her "pigeon," her "bow-wow."

Her "bow-wow" was one of the greatest generals Russia ever had; and yet he was afraid of the noise of guns and trembled like a school girl whenever a cannon was fired. Potemkin and his soldiers engaged the Turks in battle and took from Turkey vast areas of land which they annexed to Russia. Catherine was delighted. She put Potemkin in charge of developing this newly acquired territory. Potemkin made plans on paper for a new metropolis on the banks of the Dnieper River, which was to rival St. Petersburg in the north. He named it Katerinoslav—"Catherine's Glory." This so delighted Catherine that she appointed him, not only governor of the newly annexed province, but also field marshall, and inspector general of the entire Russian military complex.

Potemkin made frequent journeys to St. Petersburg to inform Catherine of the wonders of this new city which existed only on paper. But Catherine believed Potemkin. She also believed in all the other miracles Potemkin reported to her. She was certain there were fields of waving corn, lush meadows, villages full of contented, prosperous peasants. She really believed that in three years Potemkin had been able to create the happiest and most fruitful province of her empire out of a stretch of barren steppeland. She decided to visit the new provinces; she wanted to see Potemkin's miracles for herself. She had discovered this man, had sent him from her arms to serve the country—now she was to have her reward in seeing all that he had accomplished for her glory.

The prospect of the journey acted on her senses like wine. She was fifty-eight, but her enterprise, her vitality, her enthusiasm had never been more abundant. And apart from that, her Potemkin was surely awaiting her arrival impatiently.

Catherine set out on her famous journey in February. An army of 40,000 men was entrusted with the safety of the royal retinue. Catherine's sled was the size of a small house. It had little windows in each wall and was drawn by eight horses. At every station along the route five hundred fresh horses were waiting. A short distance along the road huge bonfires were lit at night. In this way the journey to Kiev was accomplished within the short space of two weeks.

They had to wait in Kiev till the ice went out on the Dnieper River. In May the queen and her immense entourage were able to embark on waiting boats. Seven floating palaces followed by eighty attendant vessels carried a total of 3,000 people. The empress's galley and those of her guests were lined with costly brocade; the walls gleamed with gold, there was gold on the servant's uniforms; and the meals were served on plates of gold. A flotilla of little boats darted among the vessels, transporting visitors from one to another, conveying wine, food, and bands of musicians who played at the numerous dinners, balls, and concerts which were arranged to amuse the floating city of high-spirited travelers.

On the river banks they glided past she saw villages painted and decorated. She saw cattle grazing in pastures, troops maneuvering in fields, and when dusk fell, peasant men and girls in their gay, fluttering costumes dancing with carefree abandon. She did not know that this pleasant fairyland vanished the moment her band had passed.

Potemkin was surely the P.T. Barnum of Russia. The gullible victim of his deception was none other than the Great Catherine and Joseph II. Potemkin had not made a garden out of the desert in four years. He had not grown forests where there had been only prairie, or created wealth where there had been only squalor. But in a very short time he had created the illusion of all this for Catherine's delight.

The inhabitants of all the towns had been ordered to put a fresh coat of paint on their houses, but only the sides that face the street or river were painted. Broken-down roofs had

been repaired, not with tiles but with cardboard painted to
imitate tiles. Potemkin had trees transplanted to screen those
unsightly places he couldn't change. These trees flourished a
few days, and after Catherine had passed they slowly with-
ered. The cattle she saw grazing had been brought in from
great distances and would be on their way home as soon as she
had passed. The population was instructed to wear its best
clothes. The girls were instructed to comb their hair, wear
flowers, and strew flower petals. The old and infirm and
unkempt had strict orders to remain indoors or out of sight.
How could Catherine know that the dancing men and girls
were wretched serfs hastily collected at Potemkin's orders?
They were quickly taught, not without considerable pains and
a few sound beatings, to perform their carefree capers. As soon
as Catherine had passed, they were packed into carts like a
traveling theatrical company and hurried over the steppes to
the next village, where they would once again provide the
empress with a spectacle of holiday-merrymaking.

Another thing Catherine was not aware of—Potemkin
had snatched no less than twenty communities bodily from
their homes in order to temporarily populate the provinces on
Catherine's trip. He had spent no less than seven million pre-
inflation dollars from her treasury on this extravaganza. She
was just as lavish in her show of appreciation—she built him
a palace in St. Petersburg. Into this trip of fantasy and
deception stumbled two Low-German Mennonites from Danzig.

Thousands of Germans had come to Russia in response to
her manifest in 1763, but there were no Mennonites among
them. She had settled these first settlers along the Volga
River. Now she wanted more Germans to populate these new
lands Potemkin had gotten for her. Specifically she wanted
Mennonites. She issued her Supreme Edict in 1786, while she
was making preparations for her journey to the south. Two
Mennonite delegates by the name of Heppner and Bartsch,
from the Low-German settlements by Danzig, started on their
tour of inspection at the same time. The paths of Catherine's

group and the Mennonite group crossed on the tour. Heppner and Bartsch met Potemkin who in turn introduced them to the Great Catherine and then directed them to his acres in hope they would decide to settle there. On their return trip the two Mennonites were routed through St. Petersburg where they met Catherine's son, Crown Prince Paul. They were favorably impressed by all they saw even if Bartsch froze his toes during the winter and Heppner broke a leg.

By the next fall (1788), 228 Mennonite families from Danzig were on their way to this new part of Catherine's empire. Thousands of Germans followed them, not only Mennonites but Lutherans, Catholics, and Reformed. These were the people that finally put substance into Potemkin's dreams. The area they settled would now become the bread-basket of Russia.

Four years after his meeting with Heppner and Bartsch, Potemkin died. Catherine was heartbroken. She fainted three times when she heard the news of his death, and had to be bled. She set aside 100,000 rubles to build him a mausoleum. But her new lover was jealous and could not endure the thought. At sixty-two years of age the toothless and sagging Catherine did not want to risk losing her twenty-two-year-old lover. She did nothing. One of Potemkin's other mistresses finally erected a modest tombstone.

Another five years and Catherine was stricken with a fatal stroke. She lingered painfully for thirty hours—almost an hour for each year she had reigned. She had been at the point of disinheriting her son Paul, in favor of his son Alexander. The papers she had executed to the effect could not be found, and at age forty-two, Paul was proclaimed czar.

The day after her death, Paul had his father's body exhumed from the grave in which it had been buried. He had his moldering bones, which could only be identified by one remaining boot, carried in solemn state through the street. He forced the aged and feeble Gregory Orlov to walk at the head of this gloomy procession behind the remains of the man he had murdered. Paul finally caused the skeleton to be set upon the throne, as a symbol of the legitimacy of his own succession. The empress's funeral was a double funeral, and in it the place of honor went to the husband that had been killed thirty-four years earlier. Side by side, the czar and the czarina, both born Lutherans, were censed by the priests of the Russian Orthodox Church. In this macabre encounter the still-fresh corpse of an old woman and the decayed remains of a young man were lighted by the same candles and saluted by the same mourning chants.

Paul also had the remains of Potemkin removed from his simple grave and flung into the river in St. Petersburg, "so that no trace may remain of him." He appropriated the palace his mother had built for Potemkin and used it for a horse stable. It is said he never had the stable cleaned, and when Paul was assassinated four years later, it was the filthiest building in all of Russia.

When the Mennonites heard of the steps Paul was taking to discredit everything his mother had done, they became concerned about their status in the new regime. Since it was Catherine that had given them their special privileges, they feared these too would now be discredited. They sent a delegation to St. Petersburg. Maybe Paul remembered his visit with Heppner and Bartsch. Whatever his reason he signed a new extension of the Supreme Edict. The copy that was given to the Volhynian Swiss is now being kept in a house on my block, here in Freeman. The copy given the Chortitza colonists was carefully kept in a vault in the archives of the colony. It, with many other important documents, was used for wrapping paper by the Bolshevists in the early days of the revolution.

After the assassination of Paul I, his son, Alexander I, ascended the throne. Again the concerned Mennonites petitioned their new czar for a reaffirmation of their special privileges, again the new ruler signed an agreement.

One of the oldest Mennonite congregations in existence met Czar Alexander I on their way to the Molotschna (Milk

River) in south Russia. The czar was on one of his inspection trips among his subjects. When he learned of the destination of this band of Mennonites, he wished them well in German— "*Leben Wohl.*" The pilgrims were so impressed that when they built their new settlement they named it "Alexanderwohl." In 1874, when this group left for America they numbered over 800 souls. The church their descendants worship in, in Kansas, still commemorates that long ago meeting with Alexander I—they still call it the Alexanderwohl Church.

The Mennonites and other Germans from Russia considered Catherine the Great a "good" queen because she invited the Germans into Russia. They consider Alex II, son of Alex I, an evil ruler because during his reign their special privileges were revoked. It might be that the Germans are guilty of poor judgment in both instances. We have seen enough of Catherine to know that she was exceptionally immoral. On the other hand, Alex II was the great liberator, the Abraham Lincoln of Russia. He was the man that finally had the courage to free the serfs. To protect the liberated serfs, he had to curb some of the privileges of the special interest groups—groups like the nobility, the Orthodox Church, and the Germans. All groups, including the Germans, were outraged. A third of the Mennonites left for America and Canada before the decade was out. It is reported that Czar Alex II was brought visibly to tears in losing such exemplary citizens. Russians that couldn't leave started to conspire against the czar. If they were captured they were executed. A bomb set off under Alexander's carriage claimed his life in 1881. The royal family built a cathedral on the place where he was assassinated. To this day the Russians pour red paint on the spot where his blood was shed. When his tomb was opened forty years after the assassination it was empty.

After his exile by the czar, Cornelius Jansen set about creating a favorable climate in America for those Mennonites that would follow him from Russia. He cultivated contacts with

powerful railroad executives, legislators, cabinet members and
even President Grant.

Grant of course was not the first American president to
mingle freely with the common people. Neither for that matter
was President Lincoln. But I believe that Lincoln best symbol-
izes the difference between our American elected officials and
the hereditary rulers of Europe. Lincoln surely was the most
common of the common people before he attained his high
office. Even when he was at the pinnacle of his power he
remembered his humble beginnings and understood the
common man and respected him. We know this because it was
Lincoln who said, "God must have loved the common people
because he made so many of them."

Jansen was surprised by the plain apparel of state and
federal officials. When he and his son went to visit President
Grant his son wrote, "We associated a government official with
a uniform and lots of gold lace and trimmings. The higher ones
would always have guards of soldiers at the entrances of their
quarters and residences. Imagine our surprise when we
reached the 'White House' to find its portals guarded by a
single colored man, who not even displayed a sword."

What struck Jansen even more forcefully was the absence
of servants in America. The Jansen family noticed this time
and again. They were shocked by it especially when they
visited the White House. Secretary Delano and the President
of the United States told them of their experiences on the
farm. The secretary casually remarked that in his younger
days he had been in the habit of milking twenty cows mornings
and evenings, and President Grant chimed in to say that he
could still hitch up and drive a team of horses as well as ever.
The Jansens were astounded. Later Peter Jansen, son of
Cornelius, remarked about this experience: "You, who never
knew life in Europe, and especially in Russia, can hardly
imagine our surprise when these gentlemen gave us the
impression that it was the usual thing for the highest official

of the United States and the Minister of Agriculture to do manual labor."

Three of the Mennonite delegates that came to spy out the land in 1873 also got to meet Grant. Tobias Unruh too noted the lack of adornment and uniforms. He wrote that the president of the country was a plain man, warm, and very friendly. Lorenz and Paul Tschetter had the same impression. Paul Tschetter noted in his diary the warmth of their reception and especially the warmth and friendship of the final handclasp.

It would seem that President Grant and his peers signaled a trend. It was a social trend in which the piety of the plain people and the autocratic manners of the aristocracy were modified. As this century slips into history, it has become increasingly difficult to distinguish the princes and potentates from the plain people.

Pioneering in Dakota Territory

An address delivered on August 6, 1982, at the International Convention of the American Historical Society of Germans from Russia in Wichita, Kansas. It was later presented under the title "Pioneers in Petticoats" at the Fifteenth Dakota History Conference, April 7-9, 1983, Dakota State University, Madison, South Dakota.

To tell of the pioneering experience in Dakota Territory is no simple task—not even for simple people. One can easily latch on to any one of many, many pioneering experiences and develop it to the point where it seems to typify the entire pioneering adventure. But there is no *one* event that describes these first, most difficult years.

For example, I could spend all of our time telling you about Chief Baboon and the grief his mischief caused for a small group of Germans from Russia in the Loretta settlement near Avon, South Dakota. Though it may be interesting, it is not typical. Our forefathers avoided undue contact with the Russians in Russia and for the most part were just as adept at avoiding contact with the native Americans in America.

Most assuredly grasshoppers were an abomination. The havoc they wrought was real enough, but an undue emphasis can easily develop a distorted picture. Terrible as they were, grasshoppers plagues were temporary. There are other problems that wouldn't go away.

The rabbit, a delight in "Hasenpfeffer" and an annoyance in the garden, was a pest in South Dakota. When men talk about rabbit depredations, they are concerned about rabbit population, density of rabbits per acre, rate of reproduction, total loss per annum, cost per acre, cost per capita, and all manner of impressive trivia, which are forgotten as soon as heard. But my grandmother—with one story—could make you remember rabbits forever. This is her story:

One of our families had a garden that was very fertile. The garden did so well because it had been planted near a stream that flowed through the property and could be watered every day. One day the mother went to work in the garden. One of her sons was badly retarded, so she took him with her. To keep him out of mischief she picked a large pumpkin and told the boy that it was a donkey egg, which just might hatch a young donkey if he would carry it up the highest bluff along the creek and incubate it by sitting on it. The stratagem worked for a while till the boy got restless. As he changed position the pumpkin got away from him and started rolling down the hill. It continued to gather speed till it hit a large rock behind which lurked a Dakota jackrabbit. When the pumpkin exploded, the startled jackrabbit took off, large ears fanning the air. Quick as a flash the boy took after him calling, *"Hee Haw Esel, Ich bin deine Mutter"* (Hee Haw donkey, I am your mother).

Now if one grandmother with one story could put rabbits in their proper place, surely several grandmothers with their stories could put the entire Dakota pioneering experience in its proper perspective. Since grandmothers have traditionally been the guardians of faith and tradition, they must have pioneering tales in their repertoire of stories. Let us consider five grandmothers and their most memorable experiences to catch the flavor of the Dakota pioneering experience.

Did grandma gamble? Perish the thought? Did grandma wager her egg money in poker sessions with the boys? Unthinkable! She wouldn't look at cards, let alone touch the devil's pasteboard playthings or let them be brought into her house. So grandma was definitely not a gambler. Right? Wrong!

When Uncle Sam bet grandma and grandpa 160 of his acres against eighteen of their dollars that they couldn't survive for five years on 160 acres of their choice in Dakota Territory, they crossed an ocean and two continents to get their ante in the pot. They staked everything they owned and borrowed if

that was not enough. No penny ante games for them. They
played for keeps and went for broke. They bet their lives. Being
a grandfather myself, I think I can sense some of the excitement
my grandfather must have felt at the thought of moving to an
unsettled land. The sudden surge of adrenalin must have
boosted his audacity to a level his normal cautious German
restraint couldn't comprehend. Meanwhile, Grandmother's
intuition probably quickened her stoical foreboding. Instinctively she must have sensed that even if they won the 160 acres,
for her personally, it was a "no win" situation. She knew no
English but already sensed what one American writer had
written: "She is a hard country on woman and horses, which
means that men and mules can make out alright."

Grandma might have allowed the faint trace of a smile to
steal across her face at the thought of Grandpa's indignation
at being grouped with mules, but that was small consolation
for her certain knowledge that there was more. For the man had
also written: "The women wind up looking fifty when they are
thirty-seven, and fifty-three when they are seventy. It's like
they wear down to what counts and just last there, fine and
staring the devil in the eye every morning." Grandfather may
not have had any intuition, but he was not without his own
private feelings. He was in full accord with another American
writer of the time. Though pious Grandpa would never
knowingly read the writings of agnostic Ingersoll, he would
agree with him totally on this matter: "I would rather live with
the woman I love in a world full of trouble, than in heaven with
nobody but men." I like to think that Grandma knew that is how
Grandpa felt. She would need this assurance, and more, to win
her bet with Uncle Sam.

In later years, Grandmother would share with her
children and grandchildren her memories of heroic struggles
with grasshoppers, drought, and prairie fires; but her greatest
difficulty was so fraught with anguish she couldn't find the
words to describe it. Brave Grandma would do instant battle
with any of her formidable adversaries spawned by the vast

Dakota prairies except one. She could not cope with the solitude of the open spaces. The village life she had known in Russia meant neighbors. Neighbors assured her of daily visits, joys celebrated together, sorrows mourned together and confidences shared together, all on a daily basis. Prairie life in Dakota meant isolation and total solitude. Neighbors lived at a distance, and close friends and relatives had often remained in Russia.

Like as not she suffered her seclusion in a hole in the ground or a crude claim shanty. A poignant example of the utter dejection induced by the loneliness of the prairies is well illustrated in an 1880 issue of *Scribner's Monthly*. The article does not identify the woman as a German from Russia but she may well have been. Many of our German-Russian grandmothers had a similar story. The reporter questioned the man first. He recited a long litany of pioneer woes and concluded by saying, "The worst of it, though, is being cut off from other folks—it's wearing on women especially; men don't mind so much after a while; but women—women are queer you know." The reporter then asked the wife if she still longs for the old life and would like to return. Surprisingly this woman now wanted to stay, but she had a special reason:

"No," she replied, with a shade of pathos in her face and in her voice, "no, not now, not since the baby died, and we buried it out there in the garden. That was the sorriest time of all. The grave was so little and pitiful, and the prairie widened out from it so far; I hadn't ever realized how big the prairie was. And it seemed wicked like, too, not to have any funeral. But after it was all over, I felt more settled and at home you may say, and since that I've never once thought I'd care to live anywhere else in the world." She paused in a meditative way, and presently she added: "I'm always glad, though, when the grass comes in the spring to cover up the grave and makes it look less like it did that winter day of the burying."

Not all mothers responded to monumental loss with the
same kind of stoicism. Take the case of Rosina Auch. Rosina and
Christian Auch were Johannestaler. People from Johannestal
were the first Germans from Russia to come to the United
States (1852 to Sandusky, Ohio) and the first to settle in Dakota
(1873). The 1873 group stayed with friends and kinfolk in
Sandusky, while their scouts (*Kundschafter*) went west in
search of a suitable place to settle. In March of 1873 these
scouts were the first Germans from Russia to step on Dakota
soil. It had been an unusually mild winter. Wheat had been
planted in February, and everything looked nice and green. By
the end of March the scouts had convinced friends and relatives
in Sandusky that (1) it didn't snow in Dakota; (2) it didn't get
cold in Dakota; and (3) Indians didn't present a problem in
Dakota. When three train cars of skeptical Johannestaler and
their supplies arrived in Yankton on April 17, they found: (1)
they were in the second day of a snowstorm that would go down
in history as one of the worst of all time, a storm that raged
unabated for five more days; (2) Dakota was challenging Siberia
for distinction as the coldest place on earth; and (3) only two
days earlier General Custer had arrived in Yankton with 800
cavalrymen to subdue hostile Indians. Concerned Yankton
citizens had to rescue Custer's troops and the Johannestaler,
and the *Kundschafter* had to be rescued from their irate
countrymen. Almost the entire group of the Johannestaler
homesteaded about twenty miles northwest of Yankton and
called their new settlement Odessa, after the region they had
left in Russia. All that remains of Odessa is a memory.

Eight families continued on and settled near Milltown on
the James River. Earlier settlers had occupied the bottom land,
forcing the Johannestal families to settle on the bluffs. Here
they couldn't find enough water to sustain life. Early in 1874
the eight families moved once more. They settled near Martin
Creek, eight miles west of Freeman. Three of their original
homes still stand: the Schempp house, now used to store
machinery, scheduled for destruction this fall; the Lang house,

built by the Holzworths for their daughter and her husband, Gottlieb Lang, not being lived in, but could be; even much of the original furniture is still in the house; and the Bertsch house, still being lived in by members of the third and fourth generations. When Rosina and Christian Auch arrived in early 1874, they joined these eight families. They took a homestead on the quarter section next to the Bertsches.

Of the eight original families, seven were Lutherans and one was Reformed. They built a church jointly and called it *Die Johannestal Kirche*. Their fellow Johannestaler in the Odessa settlement were also Lutheran and Reformed and also built a church jointly, as they had in Russia. The Odessa church eventually became Lutheran. A certain Lutheran minister refused to hold services in the Johannestal church when he found out that a Reformed minister had preached there first. The seven Lutheran families were so agitated that they joined the Reformed church. The Reformed cause may have received an assist when the lone Reformed family donated the land on which the church stood. The church is now being preserved by the Mennonites on the campus of Freeman Junior College.

Near their church the Johannestaler started a cemetery. In the cemetery there is a large patch of lilac bushes. In the lilac bushes there stands a lone marker, marked on all four sides. The scarlet fever epidemic of 1886, in the month of March, in two weeks took from Rosina Auch: Elisabeth, March 9; Magdalena, March 13; Andreas, March 17; and Christian, March 26. Unlike the mother in our story, Rosina was not drawn close to the homestead by the fresh graves. Would her attitude have been different if her children had been laid to rest in her garden instead of the new cemetery? The cemetery is only half a mile from her house. Her hair turned completely white in just a short period of time. To escape the haunting memories of the unhappy homestead, Rosina and Christian moved to Menno the same year. They bought a clothing store, although they had no practical business experience whatsoever. They soon sold the store and moved back to the farm. For retirement they moved back to Menno. When Rosina died, her husband moved back to the farm for the last time. He lived there with his youngest son till he died at the age of eighty-six. A grandson, Ken Auch, started the Homestead Chapter of AHSGR in Yankton, so that we can all remember what Rosina couldn't forget.

Not all battles on the prairies were lost, but victory often cost physical wounds that were as painful and long-lasting as Rosina's emotional scars. Take the case of Lizzie Graber.

Lizzie Graber is one of my people, a small group that originated in Switzerland, fled to the Palatinate, from there to Galicia, on to Volhynia, and in 1874 to Freeman, South Dakota, and Moundridge, Kansas. To my knowledge we are the only Germans from Russia with the Amish background. With such pious credentials one would assume we all lived in peace and tranquility. Such thinking is like heaven. It is something to be hoped for but not to be realized on this earth. The old-timers couldn't even agree on the cause of the fire that affected Lizzie Graber's life. Some said the fire started in some corn stalks that had been placed against the Russian oven to be dried for fuel. Others said that a pail full of ashes that had been removed from the oven had ignited the fire. Others insisted that it was none of the above. There were even differing opinions about the events during the fire. To maintain a neutral position, I'll not relate any of the local versions. I'll read the article in the August 1882 issue of the *Herald of Truth*. The report was submitted by Andreas Schrag, one of the twelve Mennonite delegates that scouted the country in 1873:

I have a sad accident to report, which occurred the 13th of July. The family of Peter and Elizabeth Graber were severely afflicted by fire. The children were alone in the house while their mother had gone into the garden to get something. Soon the oldest child came running and calling out that the house was on fire. The mother ran to rescue the other two children, who were still in the burning building, but the fire had already spread so far that she could not enter by the door; so she stove in a window, and in great danger to her life brought out the children: but the youngest, which was only ten months old, was badly burned in the face. In rescuing the children the mother's clothes caught fire. She extinguished the flames in front, and ran to the nearest house, which was about seventy or eighty rods distant, but there was no one at home when she came to the house. In her anxiety and excitement she had not noticed until then that the clothes on her back were on fire, and with great difficulty she succeeded in extinguishing the fire, but not until she was fearfully burned. The whole face, the hands, the whole back, the body in front appears like raw flesh. A hole is burned into her side that the ribs were to be seen. The Lord knows whether she can survive.

Survive she did, but recovery was slow and she carried the scars for life. From then on she was known as *"die verbrennte Lies."* In spite of the agony her rescue of a baby caused her, she never lost her concern for the young, not only her own but all of those in the community. This is best exemplified by another incident in her life which refuses to be forgotten.

One Sunday afternoon she glanced out of her window and saw a group of young boys marching by her place with guns at ready. The one nearest the house was "der kleine Charley." What was this world coming to? Mennonite boys hunting and on the Holy Sabbath yet! What to do? Her Amish background gave her a ready solution. They must be reported to the church elders for loving admonition and chastisement. Tradition and concern gave her no choice. However, there was a slight problem. She didn't know who the boys were! She rushed to the door and called out, *"Bube, wer sind ihr dann?"* (Boys, who are you?) The boys too knew the tradition, and like Verbrennte Lies, they too became mightily concerned. They knew precisely what this old grandmother was thinking. Quick as a flash,

Kleine Charley replied, "*Oh, wir sind Englische von Parker*" (We are English boys from Parker). So great was Verbrennte Lies's relief at finding out that these were infidel Yankees and not good German boys desecrating the Sabbath, she clasped her hands in her burned breast, turned her face heavenward and fervently exclaimed, "*Gott sei Dank! Gehen euch!*" (God be thanked! Go!)

We have seen that some grandmothers suffered for personal concerns, others suffered because of concern for their children. We will see that some paid a terrible price because they were concerned about their husbands. Take the case of Mrs. Goosen from the area around Menno and Friesen where Kassel and Heilbronn rub shoulders.

The Kasselers, as the name implies, came from Kassel in the Glückstal district northwest of Odessa. Logical reasoning would suggest that they came to Russia from Kassel in Germany. Alas! The Kasselers are not always logical. Of the ninety-nine families that established Kassel in Russia, there was only one lone emigrant from Kassel, Germany. His name was Daniel Ficke and he became the first mayor of the new village. As mayor he received the privilege of naming it, and he named it after his home city. By the time they got to the Dakotas, however, all the Alsatians and Württemberger from this village thought they were Kasselers. They continue to be reckless with the application of the name to this day. When my oldest daughter married a Kasseler and my grandchildren arrived, all were instantly called Kasselers. The Kasselers seem to have a history of proliferation. In Russia they tripled their population in fifty years. In Dakota they continued their expansive ways and soon formed a solid bloc from north of Freeman to south of Menno. Most belong to the Reformed church.

The Heilbronn people were Lutherans from the Crimea. They did in fact come to Heilbronn, Russia, from the Heilbronn area in Germany. One of their groups got a much better initial impression of Dakota than the first Johannestal group. But, then, they didn't arrive in a blizzard. They came to Yankton on the 4th of July and gleefully assumed that the bands and bunting, and the parades and crowds were all parts of an elaborately staged reception. They were mightily impressed with Dakota.

The Heilbronner built the Trinity church southwest of Freeman in the middle of their settlement. It was commonly known as the Heilbronn church. This became the first Missouri Synod Lutheran Church in the Dakotas. This, however, is not talked about as much as another incident that happened in this church.

The weary pioneers often dozed during the long sermons. The minister was chagrined. He devised a plan to waken the sleepy parishioners. The effective execution of his plan required the assistance of the reluctant janitor. All churches had janitors to fire up the church stoves early in the morning on cold winter Sundays. One Saturday the minister brought the janitor a box with a white pigeon in it. The janitor was to bring the box Sunday morning and sit with it on the front pew near the little boys. The minister would preach about the Holy Ghost. He would have much to say about "*der Heilige Geist*" and would refer to him often. At the proper time he would raise both arms high and say "*und der Heilige Geist.*" At that moment the janitor was to release the white pigeon from the box and watch the congregation come to life. On Sunday morning, an unhappy janitor sat uneasily on the front bench, with the little boys on the men's side. The despised box was between his legs. The minister warmed up to his subject. Finally both of his arms shot up and he sang out "*und der Heilige Geist.*" Nothing happened. He raised his arms higher and shouted louder, "*und der Heilige Geist.*" Nothing happened. An exasperated minister now raised his arms as high as possible, fixed a piercing glare at the hapless janitor and intoned in his loudest voice, "*Und wo ist der Heilige Geist?*" (And where is the Holy Ghost?) The embarrassed janitor looked at the floor dejectedly and merely mumbled, "*Der Kader hat ihn aufgefressen!*" (The tomcat ate it up!)

Sandwiched in between the Lutheran Heilbronner and the Reformed Kasseler was a Russian-German family that didn't belong to either group. This denied them the intimate fellowship accorded "kissing kin." If you weren't an insider, you were definitely an outsider. Had this family lived near Marion or Dolton they would be better remembered. Near those towns are many people with this family name. But between Freeman and Menno this family would have been forgotten long ago if it hadn't been for the wife's tragedy. Even by earning a niche in history, the first names are no longer remembered. They are known only as Mr. and Mrs. Goosen.

The day was 12 January 1888. During the forenoon the wind blew gently from the southeast. It was warm. It was a deceptively fine day for January in Dakota. Suddenly the wind changed direction, and in less than five minutes you couldn't see ten feet in front of you. The temperature dropped dramatically. In two hours it dropped to -25. As the storm struck, Mr. Goosen went to get some water and could not find his way back to the house. He continued to walk and ended up at the Fred Haar home in Heilbronn. When Goosen did not return, his wife made a mistake: she went out to look for him. The prairie doesn't permit mistakes. Goosen returned the next day to find his children in bed, because the fire had gone out. They had also pushed a table against the door to keep it from blowing open. They told their father that their mother had gone out to look for him. A search by the neighbors began. Chris Knodel accompanied by Fred Haar walked to the Gottlob Schmitgall farm. As they walked, Knodel spotted something sticking out of the snow. As he walked nearer, he could see that it was an arm. It was the frozen body of Mrs. Goosen almost covered with snow. She was found one-eighth of a mile northeast of the Schmitgall home.

Terrible as some of the winters were, summer weather in Dakota Territory could be just as devastating. Take the case of Maria Hofer Wipf.

Maria Hofer Wipf was a prairie Hutterite. When 1,300 Hutterites came to Dakota from 1874 to 1879, about one-third of them resumed their communal way of life and settled in colonies. These are known as the Colony Hutterites or *Brüderhöfer* or *Gemeinschafter*. The other two-thirds homesteaded on private farms, joined the Mennonite church, and are known as Prairie Hutterites.

An incident aboard ship when one of these Hutterite groups was sailing to America illustrates a fear common to most of our ancestors. Our rural, landlocked grandparents were deathly afraid of the ocean. One Hutterite in particular on this ship was in a constant state of agitation. The gentlest zephyr would cause him to panic. He would run to the captain for assurance that they weren't in imminent danger, that they wouldn't capsize, that their lives weren't in jeopardy. The captain soon tired of this routine. To rid himself of this hysterical Hutter, he told him that they hadn't been in the slightest danger. He assured him that if the worst should happen, the trouble would only be increased by his presence. He would be distracting the captain at the very time when he must give his full attention to matters at hand. The captain then told this man that the best way to assess the seriousness of the situation is to go down into the boiler room and listen to the men stoking the furnaces. They had sailed the seven seas for many years and can read the moods of the ocean and ship like an open book. He cautioned the Hutterite that they are a profane bunch of men and their salty language will blister his ears. This was, however, in the Hutterites' best interest, for once these men stop swearing, the situation is grave indeed. Our friend didn't have long to wait to put his theory to the test. A passing breeze stirred the waters and our Nervous Nellie was off for the boiler room. He soon returned. He folded trembling hands, turned his ashen face heavenward and fervently exclaimed: *"Gott sei Dank, sie fluchen noch!"* (Thanks be to God, they are still swearing!)

The story of Maria Hofer Wipf was brought to mind by something that happened at our AHSGR convention in Boulder, Colorado. You may remember a tour we took to the Center for Atmospheric and Oceanic Research. At the end of the tour we were given a packet of 8x10 photos. One of the pictures stopped me in my tracks. I knew that I had a brittle old news clipping at home with the very same picture. In the clipping it says that the picture of the storm cloud was taken on 28 August 1884 near Forestburg, South Dakota. The storm was spawned north of Huron, South Dakota, and cut an awesome swath of destruction all the way to Sioux City, Iowa. The clipping notes: "One can see two embryos or baby tornadoes in the making. Observers said they saw from seven to nine of these baby twisters at one time."

The lady who had given me the clipping was a Prairie Hutterite. She told me of some of her relatives near Bridgewater being killed and of their oxen being skinned. An editor from Indiana happened to be in Freeman on the day of the storm. He wrote in his paper about the Hutterites being killed. About the oxen he reported that their heads were twisted off. Who was right? Obviously someone had the wrong information. Recently I found the life story of Kathryn Hofer Tschetter, sister of Maria Hofer Wipf. I quote from her story:

The first important event that I can recollect was the death of my oldest sister, Maria, August 28, 1884. She and her father-in-law (Elias Wipf) and a little son were killed by a tornado. Those three that became victims of the storm were out in the field with a yoke of oxen with a wagon for a load of hay. They did not know that the cloud contained a tornado, for such storms were unknown to our people in Russia. The other part of the family found refuge in the cellar under the dwelling house. All the buildings were swept from the yard, but the house, though severely damaged, remained at its place. Those that were killed by the storm were found in a ravine about half a mile from the place where the storm struck them. The yoke of oxen were also found dead, with their heads torn from their bodies. This is a description of the violence of the tornado. I remember how my parents and I went to the home of my sister after the storm. The dead bodies were laid out on benches covered with white sheets. I still remember, when friends came to see these bodies, my dear father with emotion lifted the veil of those dear ones that had passed away, so the people could see them. My dear mother fainted. I was at that time not quite four years old; but that sight never left me. I also remember when we came home from the place, we had the little baby, seven months old, of my dead sister with us, and how mother placed it in the cradle sobbing, weeping, and saying, "Oh! what happened to our daughter Maria?" Mother found much consolation in the song:

Drum, liebes Mutterherz, Gebt euren Mut zufrieden
Lasst fahren Angst und Schmerz, Dass ich von euch
*   geschieden:*
Der, so mich euch gegeben, Nimmt wieder hin das Leben.

So, dear motherheart, let crushed spirits soar
Let the fear and anguish of separation vanish,
For he who gave me to you has now reclaimed this life.

As the words of a hymn consoled Maria's mother, so faith sustained all these grandmothers. Church services were one pioneer activity that was anticipated with relish. The Sunday morning services and mid-week celebrations, such as Ascension day, were moments when flagging spirits were revived and faith was renewed. However, it was more than an exercise in piety that made grandmother long for church. After the service, while children frolicked and men visited outside, grandmother remained in church, taking the pulse of her family's wellbeing. She compressed all of the last week's happenings into a few precious minutes with her married daughters. She and her sisters from another country and another time clung to each other in long embraces. Tears of joys and tears of sorrow flowed freely. She sought out her grandchildren and fondled them lovingly, as if she was seeing them for the first or last time. Sometimes these golden moments were extended a few precious hours with an impromptu dinner invitation.

When grandmother finally succumbed to the inevitable, she was taken to her beloved church for the last time. Surviving friends and relatives that had been supported by her through pioneering ordeals, now gently carried her to that place where she would finally have that peace and rest that had always eluded her. They gathered around the open grave for the final farewell, the last tribute, as the minister read in German, "Her children rise up, and call her blessed."

When grandmother accepted Uncle Sam's bet, she knew that it would be difficult to win. She understood that if she won, she was making it easier for her children and grandchildren. That her children also understood this is evident in an article in the April 3, 1893, issue of the *Yankton Press and Dakotan*. It concludes an article on prairie mothers with these lines:

> The births of the babies are about all that vary the monotony of her life.
>
> Occasionally death calls and takes from her tired arms a little life and leaves in its place an added pain in her heart.
>
> She is old and tired at thirty.
>
> When her daughters reach the age at which they could assist her, the dreary prospect of a frontier life appalls them, and they seek employment in town or city.
>
> Improvement stalks all over the frontier homeplace, but leaves no trace in the kitchen. Her pleasures are few.

The satisfaction that she is doing her best seems to be all that rewards her. She is a heroine in a calico dress, wrinkled and stoop-shouldered—a woman with a burden who never complains.

Late at night, when all the members of the family are in bed, a light will shine out across the prairie from the family living room. It is by this light that the frontier wife is doing her mending and sewing.

And it will shine out long after the occasional travel that way has stopped, and no one but the one who blows it out knows at what hour the patient burden bearer's labors cease.

Reinhold Dewald and Relief Cattle for Germany

This paper was first presented at the Schmeckfest in Freeman, South Dakota, March 1988, and published in the Journal of the American Historical Society of Germans from Russia *11 (Spring 1988): i-ii, 1-9.*

The flames of the war that had been extinguished in Europe three years earlier erupted with vigor in South Dakota in March 1921. The antagonists were former comrades in arms in the American Expeditionary Force in Europe. The object of contention was a herd of about seven hundred cattle collected mostly by Germans from Russia in South Dakota to be sent to Germany to provide milk for children. War reparations in France had depleted Germany's supply of dairy cows, and undernourished children were starving.

Certain elements considered this humanitarian gesture a treasonable act and made an armed attempt to abort this shipment. The shock waves generated by the confrontation rolled all the way to New York on the front page of *Issues of To-Day,* a weekly newspaper.

ISSUES OF TODAY

An American Weekly for Social Decency and Civic Justice
New York, Saturday, April 16, 1921

The Battle of the Cows

Detailed Story of the American Legion's Assault on the
Milk Cattle Gathered for the
Relief of German Children
Six Hundred Animals Stampeded in Night

Gangsters in Automobile Rode Among Pregnant Cattle and Opened Fire, But Discreetly Retreated when Confronted With Winchesters

This article had first appeared in the *Dakota Freie Presse* on April 12, 1921. The headline in the *Dakota Freie Presse* was more subdued, but with the exception of the first and last paragraphs, it was identical with the article that appeared in the New York paper, with one notable difference: the language was German.

Die Schandtat bei Scotland, S.D.
Ein zweiter Bericht über die Schandtaten eines Mobs beim Verladen der für Deutschlands hungernde Kinder bestimmten Kühe wurde uns zugesandt. Wir geben ihm seiner Ausführlichkeit halber gern Platz.

(A second report concerning the disgraceful actions of a mob during the loading of cows destined for the starving children of Germany was sent to us. Because of its explicitness we gladly give it space.) [Note: the first report was in the April 5, 1921, issue.—Ed.]

Since both papers carried the same article, both papers accused the American Legion of instigating the confrontation.

The *South Dakota Leader,* a Mitchell, South Dakota, paper, used even less restraint than the other two papers but only charged the Legion with being dupes of the Ku-Klux Klan. In large, boldfaced letters, the entire front page denounced the Ku Kluxers, the Ku-Klux viper, the outlaws, and mobsters.

THE
SOUTH DAKOTA LEADER
Mitchell, South Dakota, April 9, 1921
NEAR CIVIL WAR IN HUTCHINSON COUNTY
By Tom Ayres

Kansas held the stage for several weeks with
its maraudings, its mobbings, its illegal lynching of
free speech and peaceable assemblage; its tarring
of men for opinion's sake; its Ku-Klux governor
apologizing for the Ku Kluxers; its attorney general
finding a fidgety, foolish, fishy pretext for protect-
ing the outlaws, but it remained for South Dakota
to furnish the last example of Ku-Klux activities
and to come nearest the actual climax of civil war.

In another place in this week's issue of the
Leader will be found a news story from the *Mitchell
Republican* giving an account of a Ku-Klux raid in
Bon Homme and Hutchinson Counties in which
members of the American Legion took a leading part
and which nearly resulted in bloodshed.

Like most people in Hutchinson County (Freeman,
Menno, Tripp, Parkston, Kaylor, Dimock, and Olivet), the
editor of the *Freeman Courier* was a German from Russia. He
never used a headline, and he never had an editorial page. All
news items were worthy of one's undivided attention, so
headlines were redundant. Objective news reporting revealed
a glaring lack of conviction, therefore his news items were
liberally laced with editorial comment.

He was in the Yankton hospital when the trouble erupted.
He not only heard the local opinion, he also read about it in the
exchange papers. His account of the incident seems to reflect
affirmation of the stance of *The South Dakota Leader*. Like the
writer in Mitchell, he uses the words "mob" and "mobbers"
freely. He does not berate the Legion unduly but castigates
those who would use former servicemen "to pull their chestnuts
out of the fire." After all, most of the Hutchinson County
defenders in this skirmish were also Legionnaires.

FREEMAN COURIER
April 7, 1921
After coming home from the Yankton hospital he found it very interesting to read the articles in the exchanges about the trouble in Scotland with the gift cows. In some articles you could read between the lines that the writer felt more like defending the actions of the mobsters than telling them they are the breeders of bolshevism and lawbreakers, but nearly all the papers came out with words of condemnation for the action of the mobbers.

After gathering all the information from papers and other sources you can't help but conclude that the cause of the whole trouble is the ignorance of the mobbers, the inspiration from fellows whom the mobbers considered prominent men and that they were kept under the impression that the American Legion as an organization apposed [*sic*] the shipment of the cows. There seems to be a tendency nowadays for attempts to use former servicemen to pull chestnuts out of the fire for someone . . . .

Another account insists it was a gang of rumrunners that instigated the incident. In a speech to the members of the Homestead Chapter of the AHSGR, in the Little Stone Church in Scotland on May 17, 1987, a highly respected gentleman who well remembers the cattle war gave his opinions. This lifelong citizen of Scotland told of a gang of international rumrunners that had their headquarters in Scotland. They were not your small-town bootleggers but operated a cartel that smuggled booze from Canada and distributed it to bootleggers in America. To divert attention from their illegal activities and to give the appearance of being respectable citizens, they aroused the rowdy element.

In the oral history files at the University of South Dakota is a tape of a Freeman citizen who remembered the incident. There was no doubt in his mind that the trouble was instigated by the Bohemians.

Probably the calmest assessment of those turbulent times is that of Freeman banker Reinhold DeWald. Mr. DeWald was appointed foreman of the crew of about thirty men that was to accompany the cattle to Germany. Since these were dairy cows and had to be milked regularly, a large crew was necessary. He wrote a German report of the entire trip which he read to public gatherings when he returned from Europe. His choice of culprit? The devil made them do it!

He alludes to St. Mark, 5:11-12. "Now there was nigh unto the mountains a great herd of swine feeding. And all the devils that besought him, saying, 'Send us into the swine, that we may enter into them.' And forthwith Jesus gave them leave. And the unclean spirits went out and entered into the swine; and the herd ran violently down a steep place into the sea, (they were about two thousand) and were choked in the sea."

Mr. DeWald wrote as follows [translated by compiler]: *For many years I had entertained the thought that it would be nice to see Europe. But that it would happen so soon and that the dear cows would have something to do with it never entered my mind.*

It cost much toil and tribulation to gather the cattle and drive them to Scotland where many good people live—but where some are quite mad also. Before we were aware of it, we were involved with the aforementioned cows in such a way that we were the living proof of the old axiom, "Truth is stranger than fiction."

At first we were accused of being responsible for the trouble by the false accusation that one of our boys had stolen some bedding. When it became

*obvious that this dirty plan wouldn't work, the evil
demons entered the cattle and possessed them, since
there weren't any swine nearby. Luckily, we survived
with our skins unbroken, but several of the cows had
to surrender their hides to the salt treatment.*

*As you know, the cattle were finally loaded.
Practically all of us had pistols in our pockets to
hold the howling wolves of Scotland at bay. We were
glad when the train finally got under way, even if we
were threatened with reprisal if this should happen.
On the freight train things did not always go
smoothly, especially with the meals. The noon meal
often wasn't served until 3:00 p.m. and supper in the
morning.*

Since Mr. DeWald is writing to people who had participated in the conflict, he sees no need to repeat the details. It
may be well to interrupt Mr. DeWald's narrative here and
reprint the account from *Issues of To-Day* so that you may
become better acquainted with the three-day war in its
entirety.

(Special Correspondence *Issues of To-Day*)

Tripp, SD., April 10—The eastern papers seem
to have ignored the battle of the cows which was
waged at Scotland and Kaylor, S.D., against a herd
of 600 milch cows which had been donated by
northwestern farmers to supply milk to the starving
German children.

The South Dakota farmers who had promised
to send milch cows to Germany through the Dairy
Cattle Company, 123 West Madison Street, Chicago,
had been requested to send the animals to several
yards around Scotland, Bon Homme County, and
Tripp, Hutchinson County, which was accordingly
done.

The company had asked Pastor H. F. W. Gerike, who had charge of two congregations of the Missouri Synod, his own at Tripp and one at Emanuel's Creek, to supervise the work, and he devoted himself to the task with heart and soul.

On Wednesday, March 23, there were herded near Scotland 386 cows and near Tripp 280 head, when Pastor Gerike was notified that trouble might be expected at Scotland, as some of the American Legion men had sworn that no cows should be sent to Germany and had recruited a gang of ruffians with whom they threatened to march against the cows in order to stampede the herd and make their shipment impossible.

Meanwhile Mr. F. F. Matenaers of the Dairy Cattle Company had arrived in Scotland, and Pastor Gerike conducted him to the Mayor of Scotland to request him to have the cheriff [sic] delegate a number of deputies to protect the herd of the Dairy Cattle Company.

The Mayor promised to do so but failed to act, and when the blow fell on Thursday neither he nor the sheriff were anywhere in evidence.

No Pity for Mother Cows

During the night of Wednesday some twenty-five automobiles packed with men, with a number of others on horseback, suddenly swept down upon the scene and opened fire on the herd. Only four young men were on duty to guard the cattle, and they had no chance against such odds. The Legion gang began to shoot at everything in sight, having evidently planned a regular slaughter among the poor animals. Several cows were killed, many wounded and as many crippled. To make the stampede complete, the rowdies drove their automobiles among the frantic animals, running them down and breaking their legs. Many of them, specially selected for this purpose, were with calves. A number of the poor creatures in the stampede dropped their young in their agony.

That was the battle of the cows in which the Legion came off triumphantly.

In the gray dawn of Thursday morning the boys in charge had telephoned to the city and received instructions from Pastor Gerike to round up as many of the cows as possible. Men were sent to their assistance, and by noon Thursday the cows had been rounded up. Then came orders to give them a short rest and drive them to a yard about eighteen miles distant in Hutchinson County six miles from Tripp.

Pastor Gerike took charge and proceeded with the utmost caution, as renewed threats had been made that another raid would be made on the herd; but at the minister's urgent request the Hutchinson County authorities furnished him protection. By Thursday night one hundred deputy sheriffs had been sworn in and were on hand, the majority of them members of the Legion from the near-by villages of Parkston, Dimock and Fremont.

300 Men with Winchesters

The yard was turned into a stockade against possible assault. The outposts in autos were stationed at all approaches and no one was permitted to pass the lines without proper credentials. A number of defiant individuals were unceremoniously jugged.

Nevertheless, a renewed attempt was made. A flying brigade of automobiles crowded with men made an attempt to rush the lines; but at sight of the Winchesters in the hands of the defenders, the gallant super-patriots decided not to press matters and beat a dignified retreat. Meantime the governor of the State sent word that he was ready to send help, and the Deputy United States Marshal Mayer arrived on the scene and State Marshal Shanks announced his intention to be present.

By 10 o'clock Friday morning the animals had practically all been rounded up. Not counting the dead and injured animals, twenty-four cows had been stolen, and at this writing it is hoped that the guilty miscreants will be arrested and punished. A large number of the mob were captured and several were severely handled. The women of Tripp organized a brief notice and served the guards, numbering some 300 men by this time, with refreshments.

Threats were still made that the cattle would not be allowed to be put on the train, and the train was ordered to stop; but the loading was finally accomplished on Friday morning under the protection of 300 armed farmer lads, most of them ex-service men.

The train passed through places where threats had been made at double speed, and the train crew and boys in charge were prepared for all eventualities.

Another herd of 742 head is ready for shipment at Watertown, Wis., and these will be augmented by cows from South Dakota, as it has been decided to abandon the shipments from this State direct.

Appeal to Roosevelt

[The animals have since arrived safely at Baltimore, from which point they were to be shipped to Hamburg. On their arrival the American Legion at Baltimore made formal protests against the shipment, but with only the rowdy element to sustain them, nothing further has been heard of the cargo, and it is presumably on the high seas by this time.

Should any further interference of the kind described here be threatened, those in charge of shipments are advised to address their protests against excesses by the American Legion to Assistant Secretary Theodore Roosevelt, Navy Department, Washington, D.C.]

Reportedly there was a potential for trouble in Sioux City, Iowa. Mr. DeWald makes no mention of it when he resumes his narrative:

The first stop was in Savana, where the cows were milked and fed. From there it was on to Hammond, Indiana, close by Chicago. Here the cattle had to be branded. This created a lot of fun when an occasional cow was in a cantankerous mood. They charged into our midst so close to us that the seats of our trousers would have been in monumental risk for irreparable damage if there hadn't been high fences strategically placed for us to climb. Evidently the cattle looked on this diversion as a serious business. A glowing iron pressed an "A" into their cheeks as a remembrance of the America they would soon leave behind.

At this time America was suffering prohibition. Escape from restrictions on choice of libations was one of the "perks" enjoyed by these German-Russian cowboys. This is the first of several references Mr. DeWald makes of the forbidden beverage:

*In Hammond the boys were given their first foretaste of
Europe. Admittedly the substance was somewhat weak, but it
still contained 4 or 5 percent spirits, which soon became evident
in the legs of the boys and in the sidewalks, which constantly
became narrower.*

*In Baltimore we, together with the cattle, were locked into
the stockyards. The place actually thought itself as a hotel. According to the name it was a hotel. Yes, it even had "HOTEL"
printed across the top in large letters, but it still resembled a
barn more than anything else. And the chickens—they certainly
weren't fried according to mother's recipe by a long way, but no
one starved; only one got sick and two departed for the dear
hereafter.*

*On April 13 the ship finally set sail. The number 13 didn't
bode well for the future, but after lying around Baltimore for
nine days, we were glad to be on the move again. The bed had
been very hard, otherwise we might have been content to lie
around there till now.*

**Cowboys, ship's crew, and dignitaries on board the *West Arrow*. Photo
courtesy of Harriet Haar Schaeffer, whose father, Hugo Haar, is fourth
from left, back row.**

All of you who have been on the ocean know that every-thing goes well as long as the stomach functions properly, but once that organ malfunctions, all fun comes to a sudden stop. Only the fish are happy. This stomach rebellion was experienced by some of our cowboys on the first day out. The ship, West Arrow, *was a freighter, not designed to accommodate either man or beast. The cattle were shoved into their stalls with the rear ends against the outside walls, and then the entire contraption was nailed shut with boards. Can you imagine what an unholy task it was to milk the cows and get out the manure? The milkers had to crawl through this mess to get at the milk faucets. Sometimes you couldn't distinguish the milker from the all the filth that covered them.*

This experience evidently colored Mr. DeWald's *Weltan-schauung* for the rest of his life. Many years later, as he was delivering the Fourth-of-July Oration at Freeman's annual celebration, he was embarrassed by an insolent bird cruising overhead. Without breaking the rhythm of his rhetoric, while his eyes were turned heavenward, he removed the vile indignity with his handkerchief, as he fervently thanked the benevolent creator for not having given cows the ability to fly.

The weather was beautiful, and except for those who couldn't hold their heads up anymore, we could sit on the hay and watch the fish and waves. Then one day and one night there blew a mighty storm. Waves washed over the ship and shook it so mightily that some of the boys were thrown from their bunks. It has been said that what one learns in his youth is never forgotten, but in this instance, to a man they forgot how they had been rocked to sleep by their loving mothers. The more the steamer pitched, the more the young travelers awakened, and they fed the inhabitants of the deep. At that moment no one was thinking of sleep.

Before evening, winds and waves abated, and we all happily anticipated a good night's sleep. Joy turned to despair when a heavy fog embraced the ship and everything else in the vicinity. The steamer's horn shrieked so boisterously the whole dear night that even the most dedicated church sleeper was kept awake and alert the whole night through.

After eighteen days we finally arrived in Germany. In Bremerhaven we had to wait till the tide rose, and then we slowly proceeded up the Weser River through locks where Germans greeted us on both sides. We greeted them with milk, of which we had a goodly supply on hand. Till now all of the milk had gone overboard. I do not know if the fish had any need of it.

We had our pockets full of chewing gum and tossed it to the children. They shrieked, "Chocolate! Chocolate!" and bit into it with enthusiasm. Some almost choked. It didn't take long before our boys were showing some of the bigger girls how to properly use the jaw's mechanism to amuse oneself with this American confection.

On a magnificent Sunday morning we docked in Bremen and were greeted with the happy tidings that we didn't dare leave the ship all day Sunday, because on the Sabbath there was no one around to process our papers. Eighteen days on the water, and then the pillory! It was almost more than normal mortals could bear.

We had a ravenous thirst for fresh water and wanted to drink it on German soil: again disappointment. There was no water in the vicinity, and we had to be satisfied with German beer.

No one was arrested—even if some of the boys did leave the ship and seemed to wander about in a nebulous fog and did return to the ship by a circuitous route. They lay down in the old bunks to rest. Next morning all said goodbye to the dear cattle and to the ship's crew. They had treated us well.

We were shown the town of Bremen and were entertained one night by the city fathers. A certain doctor gave a speech in which he thanked the Americans for the nice and useful gift. He also cautioned us not to be misled by the seeming prosperity of the bigger cities, because the need in Germany was real, and it was great.

Bremen was also viewed from the air. Almost everyone crawled into an airplane. By such transportation things do not appear as nice as they do on good, old, mother earth. The air doesn't give the impression of being airtight, and everything that falls down has a long, long way to go. Whoever has a weak stomach will soon find it out under these circumstances, and what a shame that is, because everything is lost; there are no fish below us now.

The German government was appreciative and gave us free train passes to see the glories of Germany. The first stop was in Göttingen. This is a college town and seemingly very poor. The students can't scrounge up the necessary funds, and professors aren't too well provided for either. The surroundings seemed very poor too. There are hardly any horses to be seen, mostly just a solitary cow pulling a drag and occasionally a horse and cow hitched together. Otherwise the land is nice and seems to be in good condition. The right-of-way along the roads is clean and not full of junk, dead chickens, and cats—like in America.

In Eisenach another stop was made so we could visit Wartburg. Luther's table, chair, and bed are still as he left them, and on the wall can be seen the ink stain where he threw his ink bottle at the devil.

In Leipzig the Bürgermeister *went to much trouble to show us everything of interest and invited us into his private chambers for a snack. Till now no mere mortal had sat in these chairs, only mighty kings and potentates. In one of the cellars we were shown the room where Napoleon drank his wine when he was in Leipzig. We sat at the very same table and tried to the best of our ability to emulate Napoleon, but it stands to reason that this was utterly impossible for people who had just come from powder-dry America. The stomach was definitely too small or the eye too large.*

After this we were shown more large cities before the train stopped in Berlin, the capital city. Berlin is a beautiful, metropolitan area about the size of Chicago. There are many nice parks and streets of which Unter den Linden *is the best known. We often rested in the shade of the linden trees. German cities are much cleaner than their American counterparts. There are no decrepit houses scattered about with their broken windows, no fences that look as though they were survivors of the Thirty Years' War, and no roofs through which you can count the stars. Most of the roofs are covered with red tile, which makes a pretty sight when seen from the air. We were shown buildings that reputedly were 300 to 500 years old; that seems quite logical if you can decipher the characters scratched into those ancient stones—or couldn't the Germans write at that time? There are not many cars; the bicycle is prominent. The entire family sits on the bike. The average person is poor and must rely on his own "running gear" much more than we in the New World.*

Here we also saw poverty. We were in an area with so many destitute people that the wagons drove in and shoveled the cabbage, beets, potatoes, etc., into the kettles. This food is not for the poor but for the thousands of children here with their pale skin stretched tightly over protruding bones. Many are so stunted that they will never become fully developed adults.

Lady Frenzel of the Red Cross was very hospitable and drove us to Potsdam, the home of the kaisers—or better said, the former home. Kaiser Wilhelm is no longer here,. [It is] a magnificent place: no wonder Bill didn't want to leave. The empress had died shortly before we came, and we got to see the many flowers on her grave.

In the matter of clothing in Germany, there is not much difference from us. The ladies were very frugal with the cloth; sometimes the dresses are too short at the bottom and at other times on top. The girls take as much pride in their ankles and necks as do the American girls. It might be excused on the grounds that there the people are forced to save.

When we first walked the streets, all the girls we met looked at the ground. "What is the meaning of this?" we asked one another. "Do we embarrass them, or what is the problem?"

We discussed the matter among ourselves and decided to ask a knowledgeable, German gentleman. He laughed and gave this explanation. "They are looking at your shoes," he said. "By your shoes they can tell you are American."

Once again we held a discussion. The result was we all bought German shoes. Once we walked on German leather, the smiles were directly at the eyes, with such unspeakable effect that several of the boys now have a dear German wife and are happily married.

There are also those that have money. They often fill restaurants with noble barleycorn, and women contentedly smoke their cigarettes. This doesn't particularly disturb me. If it helps men and is good for their health, why shouldn't the ladies acquire a nicotine taste? They can't help it that they were created from a man's rib and therefore are of the same stuff.

Christ Kaufmann (left) and Hans Kaufmann from Freeman, South Dakota, were two of the men accompanying this shipment of cattle.

From Potsdam we returned to Berlin, where we were notified that all of the cowboys had to return to Hamburg immediately. The steamer West Arrow *was due to depart in a few days, and all of us had to return on it. Our papers weren't in order, and it was our only chance for free passage back home. Well! Well! We had often heard in Dakota that the Devil is on the loose in Hamburg, and now we had to find it out for ourselves. We were in a strange place without proper papers, men without a country, and we couldn't even complain, lest we invite imprisonment. We had been promised sixty days to wander about Germany, so you can imagine the chorus of songs of praise and thanks, sung by the boys in thirty keys and voices, about the American Cattle Company of Chicago and all the others who had promised more than they could deliver. The poor fellows that didn't have the money or the inclination to pay for their return trip now had to return home after only fourteen days.*

A certain Christ Kaufmann and I were far from satisfied with this, in spite of attempts to intimidate and frighten us with threats of imprisonment behind German steel and iron, which we knew was world renowned for its hardness and rigor. We still wanted to see more of this round world after that stomach-debilitating crossing. Without success we tried to get permission from three different American consuls. Even when a Miss Schneider (assistant secretary to the American consul) put everything in proper order, she could not persuade the consul in Berlin. When her wiles failed, we knew he was truly happily married.

All the American consuls gave the same advice, "Leave Germany as soon as possible." One, however, had a smidgen of decency and offered the opinion that we could roam all over Belgium without a pass. Good! We went to the Belgian consul and were graciously received in the German language. He asked us what we wanted. Upon being told we wished his permission to tour beautiful Belgium, he replied, "Your papers, please."

"That is something we don't happen to have at the present," we answered.

"Have you nothing at all!" asked he.

"All we have is our baptism certificates."

He studied them and said, "My dear sirs, these things are good when you arrive at heaven's portals, but here they don't mean a thing. Nevertheless, go through my country; no man will harm you."

With that remark he gave us a slip of paper with permission for thirty days in Belgium. And so we went from one consul to the other, like going from Pontius to Pilate. What took three days of effort had results everywhere except with the Americans, who told us they didn't want to see any more of us.

The scrap of paper is quite nice to look at with its many documentary stamps, but looks were deceiving. In some countries it invited close scrutiny, and the many references to it in the report and in letters to the *Courier* shows there was always the nagging suspicion that it might keep them from reentering the United States.

Since the tour of DeWald and Kaufmann through Europe is not germane to the shipment of the cattle, I shall omit that part of DeWald's report with the exception of those parts that deal with two constant concerns of his—prohibition and that ambiguous piece of paper from the Belgian consul.

Switzerland must have been a delight for the two men. The trains gave them another opportunity to tantalize their thirsty friends in Dakota.

The train cars are arranged differently than in the Western world. They have a class system, and first and second class are very cheap. Those cars have running boards like our automobiles. It is from these you enter your compartment, since there are no aisles down the middle. It is a good arrangement, because as soon as the train stops, a man pushes a cart alongside and calls out, "Hot sausages! Filled pastries! Beer by the bottle!" The train windows are shoved open, and the rest you

*can imagine: or can't you imagine a cold bottle of beer any-
more?"*

Mr. DeWald continues to tease his stateside friends about
their enforced abstinence. In a letter to the *Freeman Courier*
from Belgium he wrote:

*Some good horses are seen here. European countries are
still using their beer wagons; only Americans are on the water
wagon.*

In Freeman, South Dakota, many people still rely on
cisterns for water. In 1921 most of them did. From Holland,
DeWald directed the following observations to them:

*Here the people have cisterns for drinking water. The only
advantage they have over us when the heavens are not in their
favor is that they can drink beer till it rains.*

In his letter from Italy he confesses:

*I did want to say something about Italy, but that misera-
ble beer diverted me from my text. It affects one when one merely
thinks of it. . . . In Europe one drinks beer instead of water.
Water is now to be seen in the hotels or on the trains. If one asks
for water, the people think, "There is something missing in this
man's upper room."*

As all good things must come to an end, so did the travels
of these last two roaming cowboys. After they "convened a
conference," Christ flew to Bremen to take a freighter back
home in order to conserve his dwindling cash supply. DeWald
lamented:

*I, who had been appointed foreman over thirty men, now
stand alone. I had lost them all. I consoled myself with the*

thought that the cattle had been delivered to their proper destination in good order. My duty was done, and the boys were free to go where they pleased.

As the trip wound down for Mr. DeWald, and he anticipated home, the consequence of having extraordinary travel papers was much on his mind as he wrote to the *Courier:*

Today, June 30, we were in Rotterdam, waiting for the boat to London, where I expect to sail for home with my peculiar passport.

Once in London he wrote:

I made inquiries at the various shipping companies about prices and other information about a return trip to New York. As an American, I had planned to return on an American ship, but they asked for more money, took longer, and served only water to drink.
To make sure whether or not I could board the ship with my double first-class passport, I went to see our U.S. consul, who said, "I don't know what you have here, but you can go home without any question at any time."

In a letter printed in the *Freeman Courier* on July 21, 1921, he wrote:

This no doubt will be my last letter on this side of the pond. I presume the other boys are all home by this time telling the tales about their journey and how they milked the cows and threw the dead ones overboard.

Lest the reader fear that Mr. DeWald is still sailing the ocean blue with naught but beer to quench his thirst, let us conclude with this report of the return journey.

I decided to try one of John Bull's seagoing hotels which cleave the waves to New York in less than six days. True, such a trip is a floating hotel, but even here you can feel it does not rest on a firm foundation. It is in the neighborhood of 1,000 feet long, carries over 3,000 people, and has music and ample spirits for the stomach. The weather was nice with the exception of one night when it seemed the ship was trying to stand on its head. This was good for the shipping company, because half the passengers didn't come down for breakfast. I didn't miss a meal—you can't toss your money about with such total indifference.

Came back to New York just as the fight between the Frenchman Carpentier and Dempsey took place. Satan tempted me to pay an inflated price and to go there for a few miserable minutes. Dempsey soon showed who was most powerful. The Frenchman lay on the floor with a bloody nose, while 90,000 people shrieked like a bunch of maniacal demons.

To see something of the seven wonders of America, I stopped at Niagara Falls and then Detroit, where the Tin Lizzy (der Ford) is built.

So, my story comes to an end and seems to have been only a dream.

Journal Editor's Note: Some of the remarks by Mr. DeWald were taken from the report he gave after his safe return home. Others were extracted from letters he wrote and which were printed in various issues of the *Freeman Courier*.

What's the Use?

This address was presented at Freeman Junior College on the occasion of the Class of 1938 Reunion Banquet, May 1988, and is based on a journey that Reuben and Florence Goertz took through Lincoln Country.

When you measure notable events in your lifetime in increments of fifty years, you acknowledge the validity of your grandchildren's observations that grandparents are ancient relics. When those fifty years are added to the first eighteen years of investigation, discovery, and education you invested in getting that diploma, you admit to being a mature sixty-eight. If you graduated from Junior College in 1938 you will soon be seventy if you aren't there already. Is it any wonder we sometimes can't tell if our grandchildren are showing affection or concern when they are kind to us?

A grandmother complained that the cold weather affected her arthritis. Her loving grandson prayed, "Dear God, make it hot for grandmother!"

A doting grandmother made her grandson a hamburger for lunch. She was pounding away on the bottom of the ketchup bottle when the phone rang. She asked her grandson to answer it. The boy picked up the phone and advised the caller, "Yes, she's here but she can't come to the phone right now 'cause she's hittin' the bottle."

The nervous laughter we direct at the aging process does not disguise the proposition that "every man desires to live long, but no one would be old" (Jonathan Swift).

Why then do we celebrate anniversaries? Why do we remember birthdays? Why commemorate wedding anniversaries? Why do we often celebrate for an entire year on the occasion of a centennial or bicentennial and, in 1983, a tricentennial? Why have we gathered to recognize those that graduated from Freeman Academy and Freeman College fifty years ago? All of these festive reunions are reminders of the ravages of time and advancing years. Though we anticipated an invigorating reunion, we are flirting with the possibility of disaster.

Can you go home again? Not so long ago I read the account of one man that tried. "Everything was the same yet utterly different: Time had passed and the imperceptible changes of day after day had become gulfs between me and the past." (*Smithsonian,* Sept. 1982, p. 119)

"Time has passed and the imperceptible changes of day after day had become gulfs between me and the past." What or who has been altered by those little noticed changes? What or who has created those gulfs between us and the past? Without question, our physical environment at home and here at the school has changed, but even greater are the changes that have occurred in those of us who celebrate fifty years of post-graduate life.

Gone is the sprightly step that carried us forth into the mainstream of the adult world fifty years ago. Battered are those noble ideas that gave us inspiration. Bruised is the determination to improve a floundering society. Weary is a bent old body from what has often seemed like an unequal struggle with indifference and apathy. Our youth is gone, our idealism is tarnished, our energy is spent, and it seems that all that is left for us is a tired old question that has been nagging people since that long ago time when people first started asking themselves questions.

It is a question that has plagued the minds of men and women from the beginning of time.

It is a question that every one of us has asked ourselves repeatedly.

It is a question that will continue to harass every one of us through the remainder of our lives.

It will not go away!

It is a question that can be self destructive. It can destroy our initiative. It can cripple our effectiveness. It can limit our self-fulfillment.

You may well ask, "If this question is so destructive, if a satisfactory answer is so elusive, why even mention it?"

I speak of it so we will realize that you and I are not the only persons afflicted with it. I want us to be aware that the fickle finger of fate has not beckoned us alone to grapple with the doubts this question raises.

I want us to recognize this question as a normal part of the normal climate, in which we grew up and now grow old.

This presentation will not help you eliminate or answer the question. I hope it will help you recognize it as a universal affliction. Not just your own private scourge.

This question that can fill your souls with a feeling of despair and futility bothered one of the wealthiest men in the history of the world. He was also considered one of the wisest men of all time. Yet—in his old age this question continued to bother him so much that he wrote a book about it. The book is still being printed. It has been translated into most of the languages of the world. I think all of you have your own private copy of this book.

The man was Solomon, the book was Ecclesiastes, the question—three little words—What's the use?

Listen to what the writer wrote:

"What profit hath a man of all his labor which he taketh under the sun?! (What's the use?)

All things are full of labor . . . man cannot utter it; the eye is not satisfied with seeing, nor the ear filled with hearing. The thing that hath been . . . it is that which shall be; and that which is done is that which shall be done and there is no new thing under the sun!

Then I looked on all the works that my hands had wrought and on the labour that I had labored to do; and behold . . . all was vanity and vexation of spirit.

And there was no profit under the sun—What's the use?

Isn't this a dismal commentary on the value of a person's contribution to humanity? Or does your spirit, like mine, recoil at the thought and cry out, "Something must have been overlooked! An investment in a Christian education and fifty years of honest effort must have some tangible results. There must be more than vanity and vexation of spirit."

In a search for some reassurance that a properly motivated, well directed life is not lived in vain, that valiant effort is not an exercise in futility, I cast about for a role model to validate my "gut feelings." I looked for a person who had a major impact on the destiny of our country. I tried to think of a person that is universally admired and respected. I think many of you would agree Abraham Lincoln is such a man. Most of us really think that Abraham Lincoln did make a difference. So it came as a surprise to me, that he, like the writer of

Abraham Lincoln

Ecclesiastes, spent his life wrestling with the question—What's the use?

Abraham Lincoln's own words, as written by Carl Sandburg, paraphrased the sentiment. In life his intellect was challenged by the question, and only his death gave respite from nagging doubt—What's the use?

I invite you to walk with me where Lincoln walked, to assess the weight of his burden, to ponder the depth of his dilemma, What's the use?

Abraham Lincoln was born on February 21, 1809, in a little log cabin in a clearing in the Kentucky woods.

The Lincoln family in some parts of the country was prominent, but this branch had come down in the world.

The cabin was a ramshackle affair. The clearing in which it was built was rank with weeds. The few acres of corn that stretched away to the forest were choked with grass.

The father, Thomas Lincoln, was a carpenter but seems to have neglected his trade to wander through the woods, gun in hand and dog at heel.

To the kind mother, Nancy Hanks Lincoln, was left almost the entire care of the little clearing. To the wonderful energy and the brave cheerfulness of this woman Lincoln owed the incentive of his life. "God bless my mother," he said in later years, "All that I am or ever hope to be I owe to her." She would have been happy to hear this, for she too had heard the question, "What's the use?"

Though Nancy Hanks Lincoln brought inspiration into young Lincoln's life, she did not bring honor. She didn't know who her father was. Her mother didn't know who the father was.

Lucy Hanks, mother of Nancy Hanks Lincoln, maternal grandmother of Abraham Lincoln, was indicted on November 24, 1789, by a grand jury in Mercer County Court, for loose and shameless conduct with men. She didn't even know who sired her daughter, the mother of Abraham Lincoln.

When confronted with this stigma, illegitimate Nancy Hanks Lincoln might well have asked, "What's the use?"

It does seem surprising that a person of such questionable lineage would have his birthplace preserved in a marble sanctuary. All the more remarkable because not only was he denied the blessing of proper progenitors he was bereft of a pleasant appearance. He was ugly!

When he was given to an elder cousin to be held and cuddled, the cousin took one look and handed baby Lincoln to an aunt. "Aunt, take him," she said, "He'll never come to much!"

His own father lamented when Abe was a young man, and said, "He looked as if he had been rough-hewn with an ax and needed smoothing with a jack-plane."

Strangers thought when they looked at him, "This man is a clown!"

Newspaper editors wrote of him as a gorilla.

Even in death his admirers found it hard to find nice things to say about his appearance. Wrote one about Lincoln in his coffin: ". . .His belongings were nothing . . . Dignities would not stick to him. . . . His personal qualities protrude from his official court dress as the bones of his great hands did from his kid gloves. The undertakers could make nothing of him. He was a character . . . not a doll. The decorators tried their hands on him in vain!"

Wrote another: "A character so externally uncouth. . . . So pathetically simple. . . . So unfathomably penetrating. . . . So bizarre, grotesque, droll, wise, and perfectly beneficent."

Surely ugly Abe Lincoln of tainted lineage and unpleasant appearance had ample reason to ask, "What's the use?"

Again there were quiet and anxious days in 1812 when another baby was on the way. Again came neighbor helpers and Nancy gave birth to her third child.

They named him Thomas but he died a few days after, and Abe's sister, Sarah, and Abe, saw in a coffin their father made, the little cold still face and made their first acquaintance with death in a personal grief in their own one-room cabin.

Lincoln's father was of a wandering disposition, and when Abraham was seven years old, the father moved his family to a farm in Indiana, then almost a wilderness.

Here the Lincoln family crossed the river from Kentucky to Indiana. We couldn't cross here.

We followed the river to this place, were ferried across, and again picked up the Lincoln trail.

Here, in the late autumn, father and mother and son set to work with their axes to make a clearing in the woods for a new home.

Winter was almost upon them, and with more haste than care they built themselves a half-faced camp of logs, an open lean-to to shelter them in the winter.

In the autumn of 1818 a strange sickness broke out all over the countryside, killing men and cattle by the dozens. Mrs. Lincoln was among the ones stricken. A week after she was taken ill, her husband and son, with heavy hearts, built the rough, pine coffin for the wife and mother who had loved them so well and served them faithfully.

While Thomas Lincoln whipsawed a log into planks for her coffin, young Abe silently whittled wooden pegs to serve as nails for the crude box.

Together they buried the wife and mother in an unmarked grave near Pigeon Creek.

The marker does not mark the grave, just the approximate site of the final resting place of one who in life must have asked often, "What's the use?"

The state of Indiana erected a memorial to Nancy Hanks Lincoln, illegitimate daughter of Lucy Hanks, burdened wife of itinerant Thomas Lincoln, mother of ugly Abraham Lincoln . . . because this unattractive son would not accept what seemed to be the obvious answer to the obvious question, "What's the use?"

At twenty-one he left his father's farm for New Salem, Illinois, a village of twenty cabins and 100 inhabitants, his home for the next five years.

Lincoln called himself "a piece of floating driftwood, accidentally lodged at New Salem."

Here he ran for the Illinois legislature and lost the county election.

We went to New Salem at night and followed Lincoln's footsteps by the light of a moon so bright you could read by it—but not bright enough to take pictures.

When we spoke to each other it was in whispers, for the spirit of Lincoln strolled with us.

He looked over our shoulders as we peered through the windows of the Mentor Graham house.

Before Graham came to South Dakota to live, he helped Lincoln study Blackstone and become a lawyer.

We peeked into the store where a no-good partner caused bankruptcy. Lincoln assumed the burden and repaid the creditors in fifteen years.

We passed by the tavern where Lincoln developed as a speaker in frequent debates.

There was another presence we felt almost as much as we felt Lincoln. It was that of a young girl.

Lincoln's deepest attachment in New Salem was Ann Rutledge, a lovely auburn-haired girl of eighteen when Lincoln first met her. She looked with sympathy at the gaunt young man of the people.

They were going to get married, but the chills and fevers of malaria came to New Salem in the spring of 1835. Ann was buried at twenty-two.

For weeks Lincoln roamed the countryside like one who had lost his reason. After finally finding one person who could look on him with favor and love him, she died.

He surely must have repeated the question, "What's the use?"

Dripping with melancholy, he packed his worldly goods in two saddlebags and rode to Springfield, the state capital twenty miles away. He never returned to New Salem again.

In Springfield he entered a law partnership and applied for the office of the United States Land Office. The job was given to his worst enemy.

He became a candidate for the senate . . . and lost.

He wanted to be Vice-president of the United States, only to succumb to defeat once more.

He retired from politics; there was no positive answer to the question, "What's the use?"

Lincoln bought a house . . . the only one he ever owned. He became engaged to Mary Todd. Shortly after they were engaged, Abe told her he didn't love her enough to marry her. She started to cry. So he took her in his arms . . . and kissed her and said he was sorry.

The wedding day was set for January 1, 1841. The wedding cake was baked . . . the quests were assembled . . . the preacher was there . . . but Lincoln didn't appear.

His friends found him at daylight mumbling incoherent sentences. He had become dangerously ill in body and ill in mind.

He said he didn't want to live; he wrote a poem about suicide and had it published in one of the Springfield papers. He thought he had found the answer to the question, "What's the use."

Lincoln wrote a letter to his law partner who was then in congress. "I am now the most miserable man living. If what I feel were equally distributed to the whole human family, there would not be one cheerful face on earth. Whether I shall ever be any better I cannot tell. I awfully forebode that I shall not. To remain as I am is impossible. I must die or be better it seems to me."

For almost two years after that, Lincoln had nothing whatever to do with Mary Todd. Then a self-appointed matchmaker in Springfield brought them together. Mary Todd told Lincoln it was his duty to marry her. Lincoln understood duty . . . he married her.

He was very fond of his four children . . . then one of them died.

He came out of political retirement and became our president. Because of the many candidates he was elected with only forty percent of the vote. Sixty percent of the people were opposed to him.

By the time he was inaugurated seven states has seceded. His predecessor did nothing. His detractors decried Lincoln as a "Nullity," a maker of clumsy jokes, a third-rate country lawyer who resembled a gorilla.

To preserve the Union, the new president who had once said, "Isn't it strange—I never could cut off a chicken's head," found himself embroiled in a catastrophic civil war and the bloodletting of 700,000 American men.

His new home in the White House was not a sanctuary. His country's problems followed him home. His wife was a nagging shrew who threw hot coffee in his face. Another of his sons died.

Lincoln was disinclined to go to the theater party planned by Mrs. Lincoln. A third rate drama, *Our American Cousin,* was showing at Ford's Theater. And Mrs. Lincoln had set her heart on it.

That afternoon he had told an aid about the theater party: "It has been advertised that we will be there and I cannot disappoint the people. Otherwise I would not go . . . I do not want to go."

Out in a main-floor seat Julia Shephard is writing a letter to her father about this Good Friday evening at the theater.

"Cousin Julia has just told me that the President is in yonder upper right hand private box so handsomely decked with silken flags festooned over a picture of George Washington. The young and lovely daughter of Senator Harris is the only one of his party we see as the flags hide the rest. But we know Father Abraham is there like a father watching what interests his children. We are waiting for the next scene."

The next scene is one of the most incredible and chaotic that ever stunned an audience. A one-shot brass derringer, a little eight-ounce weapon, sends a lead ball into the anterior lobe of the left hemisphere of Lincoln's brain.

As the assassin leaps to the stage his spur catches on the bunting. It throws him off balance and he breaks his leg. In the confusion he makes good his escape by hobbling to a waiting horse back stage.

With one doctor carrying Lincoln's head, another the left shoulder, a third doctor the right shoulder, and four soldiers supporting the legs and trunk, they carry him into the street. Across the crowded street, a man standing in a doorway with a lighted candle beckons.

In the rented room of a boarding house, Lincoln is put on a cornhusk mattress resting on rope lacing. The long knee elevation troubles the doctor. He orders the foot of the bed removed. This cannot be done. The doctor now has Lincoln moved so that he lies diagonally across the bed, and propped with extra pillows. He is gently slanted with a rest for the head and shoulders, finally in a position of repose.

Out of a monotonous gray sky a cold rain begins to fall. The last breath is drawn at twenty-one minutes and fifty-five seconds past 7:00 a.m. on Saturday, April 15, 1865.

A special train slowly took him back to Springfield, to a special burial place, near to the first and only home he had ever owned.

Would the peace and tranquility that had been denied this man in life now be his in the grave? It was not to be.

A large minority of Protestant ministers made reference to the death in a play house. Said one, "Our lamented President fell in the theater. Had he been murdered in his bed, or in his office, or on the street, or on the steps of the capitol, the tidings of his death would not have struck the Christian heart of the country quite so painfully. For the feeling of the heart is that the theater is one of the last places to which a good man should go."

Said another, "Would that Mr. Lincoln had fallen elsewhere than at the very gates of hell."

A gang of counterfeiters tried to steal Lincoln's body from his tomb. With the coffin half out of the grave, they were apprehended.

There was no law in Illinois against stealing a body, so they were indicted and tried for conspiring to steal a coffin, worth only $75.00.

After Mrs. Lincoln left the White House, she got so deeply in debt she sold her dead husband's shirts with his initials on them.

A grateful nation finally showed its respect and approval by erecting a monument in the nation's capital. Chief Justice Taft said, "Here on the banks of the Potomac, the boundary between the two sections whose conflict made the burden . . . the passion . . . and the triumph of his life . . . it is peculiarly appropriate that it should stand."

Wrote another, "He hoped little, expected nothing. A man of low temperament and sad nature. He worked and waited, waited and worked. Bearing all things, enduring all things. But neither believing all things . . . nor all things happening. Bearing and enduring, oh, how much even from his friends.

"What a history was written on that care-worn and furrowed face . . . of suffering accepted, sorrow entertained, emotions buried, and duty done."

Did the agony of Lincoln's hours obliterate his great contributions? Was the question that gushed from his despair legitimate? Could he on good faith ask, "What's the use?"

Three million five hundred voices of affirmation were heard in the plaintive songs of thanksgiving from the freed slaves.

Seventeen thousand Mennonites, including many of our grandparents, indicated approval by responding to the Homestead Act Lincoln signed in 1862.

He didn't live to hear the grateful slaves, he didn't see the rush of our ancestors in response to his invitation.

I do hope he did have the opportunity to read the words on a scrap of paper found in Old Saint Paul's Church in Baltimore, in 1692, 118 years before he was born.

These words speak not only to President Lincoln; they have much relevance for those aging pilgrims who graduated from the halls of academia fifty years ago, those who are graduating now, and anyone else who may have asked, "What's the use?"

Go placidly amid the noise and haste. Remember what peace there may be in silence!

As far as possible—without surrender—be on good terms with all people.

Spread your truth quietly and clearly, and listen to others, even the dull and ignorant. They have their story to tell.

Avoid loud and aggressive persons, they are a vexation to the spirit.

If you compare yourself with others you may become vain and bitter. For always there will be greater and lesser persons than yourself.

Enjoy your achievements as well as your plans. Keep interested in your own career, however humble. It is a real possession in the changing fortunes of time.

Exercise caution in your business affairs, for the world is full of trickery. But let this not blind you to what virtue there is. Many persons strive for high ideals and everywhere life is full of heroism.

Be yourself, especially do not feign affection, neither be cynical about love. For in the face of aridity and disenchantment, love is as perennial as the grass.

Take kindly the counsel of the years, gracefully surrendering the things of youth.

Nurture strength of spirit to shield you in sudden misfortune . . . but do not distress yourself with imaginings. Many fears are born of fatigue and loneliness.

Beyond a wholesome disciplining—be gentle with yourself! You are a child of the universe . . . no less than the trees and stars. You have a right to be here, and whether or not it is clear to you, the universe is unfolding as it should.

Therefore, be at peace with God, whatever you conceive Him to be, and whatever your labors and inspirations in the noisy confusion of life . . . keep peace with your soul.

With all its shame, drudgery and broken dreams, it is still a beautiful world! Be careful. Strive for happiness.

The Goertz Collection

Given November 12, 1988, Center for Western Studies annual meeting. Shortly after, Reuben Goertz suffered a ruptured aneurysm. At the time of this talk the collection had not yet been deposited at the Center—as it is now.

When, as a child, your only language is an obscure German dialect, spoken only in two rural Mennonite churches in southeastern South Dakota, and in three rural Mennonite churches in Kansas, you learn about cultural shock the day you start school. In 1924, practically the entire first grade in Freeman Public spoke German as their first language, but only my teacher and a few of my classmates spoke my peculiar Palatine dialect. I was a minority within a minority.

Kitty-corner across the block from my home lived my paternal grandmother. My German grandparents had come to America, from Russia, in 1874. My barely literate grandmother sensed that in due time the heat of the American melting pot would burn off the edges of our unique sub-culture. The distinctive flavors of my German dialect, my Mennonite religion and Russian-German lifestyle would be lost in the swirl of the stirring spoon. All too soon I would be American—not German.

This, Grandmother knew and understood, but she would not accept a rejection of her cultural identity by her grandchildren.

As the spider spins its web to hold its victim, Grandmother bound me to my heritage by skillfully weaving an imaginary tapestry, embroidered by the tales of the heroics of kinsmen from the Reformation to the present. An odyssey from Switzerland and Friesland to Germany, Russia, and finally Dakota Territory. A saga of cruel reversals and minor conquests. Of oppression and deliverance. Of eviction and refuge.

Always those bowed but unbroken heroes were kinsmen. Under Grandmother's spell the characters of her stories became very real, but they were faceless and obscure till my father brought out his old shoe box.

As young men, my father and an uncle of mine acquired a camera and some photo-developing equipment. The harsh realities of pioneer life did not allow much money or time for frivolous hobbies. When father ventured into matrimony and assumed family obligations, photography was abandoned forever, but the faded pictures remained.

When I repeated some of Grandmother's stories to my parents, they often responded by telling of their own memories of some of the characters and events. But the most delightful times were those when father would get out his old shoe box full of faded photos from the turn of the century and verify those verbal descriptions. Old ladies peered at me from carefully folded babushkas tied around their heads. The men were even more inscrutable because of their full beards. I was enthralled.

The agriculture and architecture of these strange-sounding, odd-looking immigrants from Russia helped alter the Dakota plains. Their rammed-earth homes and Turkey Red wheat are but two of the revolutionary concepts they introduced to this country; they like to boast about them. They choose to remain silent about the Russian Thistle.

To survive, the Germans needed to adapt to American ways as well. The symbiotic relationship that developed between old and new world methods and cultures is a part of the story.

Pietism and Prohibition were important issues for the Germans in Russia and again in Dakota. Surprisingly, attitudes toward pietism caused much more friction among this ethnic group than the concern about strong drink. The church, which should have been a source of unity for these deeply religious people in a strange land, became a major source of confrontation in America. It's a matter of record in the Collection.

Whether your sphere of interest is in the Soviet Union or South America, there should be something in the Collection to help your research. Did the Germans, especially the Mennonites, in South America offer Mengele sanctuary? Has *glasnost* reached the German-Russians in Siberia or Taschkent? Is religion still considered the opiate of the people?

Check it out!

How do you check it out?

The Collection has already been deeded to the Center for Western Studies, but it is still in my home in Freeman to enable me to finish indexing it. Since the Center for Western Studies, and the American Historical Society of Germans for Russia, headquartered in Lincoln, Nebraska, has IBM computers, I am indexing on an IBM-compatible computer. This will permit the index to be searched on my computer or on their computers. The index can be printed out on cards or paper at any of these locations. On the computer you can search by subject, title, author, etc. I estimate that the collection is about one-third indexed. Two good years should have the project current. Hopefully it will continue to grow and never be finished.

The archives of the South Dakota Conference of the United Church of Christ at the Center for Western Studies have a treasure trove of information about the Germans from Russia. This valuable resource was put into the Center when Yankton College closed. I would hope that this historical gem will enhance my collection, and my material, in turn, will help explain the importance of the ecclesiastical records to interested Germans from Russia. A short review of *The Guide to the Archives of the South Dakota Conference of the United Church of Christ,* by Harry F. Thompson, has been published in a recent journal of the American Historical Society of Germans From Russia.

What started out as a collection of stories about the odyssey of a small remnant of Swiss Amish Mennonites in two rural churches in southeastern South Dakota has been expanded into a rather comprehensive library of the entire Anabaptist movement from before the Reformation to the present time; from Zurich, Switzerland, to Freeman, South Dakota, and other remote places scattered around the world.

The photographs in Father's shoe box, along with about 6,000 other old pictures from boxes and albums in countless Freeman attics, have been copied on 35 mm slides. This collection of old photographs has been augmented with hundreds of newer pictures of places of interest to Germans from Russia, taken on two tours along ancestral trails in Europe and Russia, and one tour among the Germans from Russia in South America.

The events that shaped the lives of my ancestors were shared in most instances by many non-Mennonite Germans. The internal pressures in Germany that caused my forefathers to leave established homes, and the special inducements that lured them to Russia, did not affect Mennonites alone. Catholics and Evangelicals (Lutheran and Reformed) reacted to German repression and responded to Catherine the Great's invitation before the Mennonites did. When Alexander II revoked the privileges in 1871, many of all faiths in the German communities in Russia left in droves. Their story reflected my story. Their history echoed my history. Their literature became my literature.

Of the 120 lineal feet of shelf space in my book collection, about 20 feet hold books about Russia and her German subjects. Another 30 feet of shelving have books about Mennonites and their Russian experience. Since books about Russia and her natives are germane to a comprehensive study of the Russian-Germans, it follows that books of South Dakota and her natives are important too. Books about Russian and South Dakota history abound.

Books about South Dakota history occupy many shelves in the Collection for obvious reasons. The many books about the Native Americans may call for a brief explanation. The plight of the American Indian in the 1870's disturbed some of the more tender Mennonite consciences. Early success in mission fields with the Cheyenne, Arapaho, and Hopi generated encouragement. Since these are not local Indians, the Mennonite Indian interest is rather broad in scope.

In addition to the books and pictures there are twelve 24-inch drawers of vertical files, plus six large drawers full of odd-sized material about Mennonites, Germans from Russia, the countries where they lived, and the spiritual and physical environment in those places—past and present. The Collection admittedly started with a Mennonite bias but has outgrown much of its parochial emphasis.

The most difficult problem for some who would use the Collection is the language of some of the books and documents. Many of the older ones are in German, and a few legal papers are in Russian. Practically all of the Russian items and some of the German ones have been translated. Hopefully there will always be German students available to help with the German material that hasn't been translated yet.

Those who would use my Collection must presently call at my home. If you forget my name or town, call the Center for Western Studies, or the American Historical Society of Germans From Russia, and they will put you in touch with me. A generous attitude about the sharing of information is what drew me to the Center originally. The constitution defines the purposes and goals in part by the desire "To establish the existence of the Center in the consciousness of the academic community and the people of the region surrounding the College, and to build cooperative relationships with organizations having related interests."

This is not an idle pledge. Newer but much more extensive than my Collection is that of the American Historical Society of Germans From Russia, in Lincoln, Nebraska. When

I signed my Collection over to the Center, Dr. Sven Froiland
and Dr. Lyn Oyos took me to Lincoln to visit with the staff at
AHSGR headquarters so I could emulate and integrate. You
can be assured that your German-Russian research gives you
access to three sources of information.

I will admit that my attempt to describe my Collection
and its genesis may have sounded autobiographical. Since it
has been a life-long endeavor, I could think of no other way to
present it. Since I wrote this, I have read an article that has a
better ending that I could devise. I will borrow the last
paragraph of that article and with a slight modification use it
here: "Of course any autobiography or dramatization of one's
pilgrimage is to some extent a fiction. One selects and orders
memory, creates the past by discovering emergent patterns
and progressions which are a part of conscious experience only
in retrospect. Therefore these vignettes from my memory of
growing up as a Russian/German Mennonite kid are true but
not the whole truth."

There is much more. For this reason I will be happy to
entertain questions.

Schmeckfest 1989

This paper on measurements and favorite stories was presented at the 1989 festival of ethnic food and culture known as Schmeckfest, held annually in Freeman, South Dakota.

Last summer the Schmeckfest Committee asked me for yet another presentation. I reluctantly promised and in turn they promised never to ask me again. Over the years, in this room, we have exhausted about every historical subject imaginable, and we have exhausted the old man that has presented them. We have discussed the martyred saints in Europe, followed German Catholic, Lutheran, Reformed, and Mennonite pilgrims to Czarist Russia, and then came with their children to South Dakota where we have observed both their supreme sacrifices and our own sullied search for the preservation of sainthood.

Last year the Cattle War in Hutchinson County following World War I was the topic. The year before we followed Laura Ingalls Wilder as she and her husband Almanzo drove by Freeman on their way from DeSmet to Missouri. Every year we settled on one subject and tried to develop it. In the process many stories were told, but many were left untold because there was no way to fit them into the matter at hand. Then there were those stories I liked so well I would like to tell them once more. Some stories were true, some sounded a little suspicious . . . but all illustrated a point. I am in complete agreement with Washington Irving: "I am always of easy faith in such matters, and am ever willing to be deceived where deceit is pleasant and costs nothing. I am therefore a ready believer in relics, legends and local anecdotes of goblins and great men; and would advise all travellers who travel for their gratification to be the same. What is it to us whether these stories be true or false, so long as we can persuade ourselves into the belief of them, and enjoy all the charm of reality?" (Washington Irving)

My wife's grandpa Gering expressed the same lengthy sentiment in one short sentence: "Never . . . but never let the truth stand between you and a good story!" —Johann J. (Hanzul) Gering, grandfather of Mrs. Reuben Goertz.

I think my attitude toward these old stories is best expressed by the well-known author anonymous. "Stories are folklore—rough retellings that aim at entertainment. Folk tales are not children's stories—they are part of the literature of a whole people. They embody the history and mores of a culture, often illustrating the sanctions and restrictions of a given society. Just as stories of bravery, generosity, piety and cleverness were told to promote these qualities, so too, were violations of community and church laws and standards told to proscribe certain behaviors. Folklore is essentially an oral art, its form and detail slowly evolving through the years."

So this last time around I would like to forego the structured format and wander about here and there with stories I have told and stories I have never told before. In the telling I hope I can demonstrate the value of these stories as a way of preserving our history and encourage you to write your stories. When our ancestors told stories many seemed to have the flavor of fairytales. Recent discoveries of pertinent old materials have proven grandparents were very good in preserving their history with their stories. Even after 200 years some of the old tales are proven very accurate:

1. Rupp burial
2. Wolves
3. Sea burial of great grandma Goertz
4. Kathryn Hanzul's death—January 6, 1981
5. Paltowitz ear
6. Hier Kissen (German to English)
7. Bull SchieBen (English to German)
8. Fine for dumping (German sentence structure in English)
9. Huggy buggy ride
10. Crazy Unruh car

11. Your heifer easier to catch
12. Now let your mama do the worrying
13. Sleep in barn

There is another vital thing to preserve beside stories if we are going to keep future generations informed of the life styles of ancestors. It is something we talk about frequently but most of us don't even know what we are talking about when we do. This is the matter of measurements. It isn't as important to know that President Lincoln signed the Homestead Act in 1862, as to know how much land was offered each homesteader. The homesteading fees were $18.00. So for $18.00 Uncle Sam was betting our forefathers that they couldn't live on a claim of land of their own choosing for five years. If they could—the claim was theirs. How much land was involved? How big was a claim?

How big is a quarter section? (160 acres)

When the Germans were invited to settle in Russia, one of the inducements also was free land. The amounts varied from time to time. When the Mennonites went into Russia they were offered 65 dessiatine of land per family head. Which country was more generous—America with an offer of 160 acres or Russia with 65 dessiatine? (dessiatine=2.7 acres x 65 dessiatine=175.5 acres)

Given all of this information, will your grandchildren now know how big an acre is? Unless they live on a farm they probably won't. We still haven't come to grips with the problem. Our grandchildren still haven't been given an understanding of the size of an acre, a mental picture of the size of great granddad's claim. One hundred sixty square rods may not mean anything to us in a few years from now if we go to the metric system. To help them understand, will you tell them an acre is as big as a . . .

	acre=43,560 sq. ft	
football field?	160x360=57,600	14,000 over
baseball infield?	90x 90= 8,100	5+ infields

basketball court?	50x 94= 4,700	9+ courts
tennis court?	36x 78= 2,808	15+ courts
Freeman city block?	300x300=90,000	over 2 acres
sheet from king size bed?	9x8.5=76.5	569.5 sheets per acre

If great grandpa wrote his friends in Russia that the first year on his claim he broke two acres of sod, planted it to wheat, and the resultant crop filled his triple box, what would this tell you about his wheat crop? Was it good or bad? How many bushels of wheat did great grandpa harvest?

Single box	14 inches @ 2 bushel per inch=28 bu.	
Double box	12 inches @ 2 bushel per inch=24 bu.	52
Triple box	10 inches @ 2 bushel per inch=20 bu.	72

There was a letter from Russia on May 26, 1908. Rye flour now goes for 1 ruble, 20 kopek per pud (pood), oats for one ruble, wheat for 1 ruble to 1 ruble 10 kopek.

We aren't concerned about the value of the money. After all, our own money changes in value from day to day. What is of concern is the size of a pud. In another letter this man wrote he had two pud of potatoes. How many potatoes are you going to tell your grandchildren he had?

Did he have two pailfuls?

Did he have two bushels?

Did he have two tons?

Did he have enough to supply the Schmeckfest?

How much is a pud? (36 pounds)

Pud rhymes with food.

Potatoes are food.

The Schmeckfest is all about food—so a few questions about food before we go dining. I have some of the answers for all of the questions I will ask except the very first question.

When mothers summoned their family to the table they wanted their food to be enjoyed. They would say, "*Wer nicht kommt zu rechten zeit, der nuss essen was ueberich bleibt.*"

We didn't need that kind of encouragement. It seems we were always hungry and the mothers were virtuosos with their pots and pans in their kitchens—most of the time. But then there were "those" days, when even the best cooks would falter. Then mother would sternly remind their children of humanitarian considerations involved in eating what was on the table with the remark, "*Die arme kinder in Rugland*" ("The poor, starving children in Russia would be delighted with this food").

If this appeal to our finer instincts didn't elicit an enthusiastic response, mother would appeal to our piety. "*Besser es esse wie Gottes gabe verachte*" ("Better to eat it than to ignore God's bounty").

Now the question whose answer eludes me is this. The meals that were so delightful made mothers smile because they reflected favorably on mother's skill, but the infrequent tasteless meals (the flops as it were) seemed to be God's providence. It was God's providence—the reasoning here eludes me.

Grandmother's meals required much preparation. (Flail)

Butchering doesn't look appetizing, but this description of America's most popular breakfast doesn't sound so inviting either.

"We relish a breakfast of the fatty tissue taken from the underside of some dead animal, the embryo of some unborn young, all washed down with a fluid secreted by the mammary glands of a beast that extracts this secretion from weeds and grass."

In those bygone days, some Freeman mothers used some rather ingenious devices to prepare their gourmet dishes. How well do you remember what food was prepared . . .

with the feet? (sauer kraut, wine)
on the knee? (kneeplez—flaetz—cookie or biscuit)
on a window screen? (snitz—dried fruit)
on a broom stick? (noodles)
on a newspaper? (dried beans)
in a barrel? (sauer kraut, pickled melons)

in a pig's intestine? (sausage)
in a pig's stomach? (swarte mage—headcheese)
in a cloth sack? (cottage cheese, jelly)
with a funnel? (wasp nest)
with a tumbler & thimble? (doughnuts—zucher cookies)

Milk was an important part of the diet. Almost all of the milk was gotten from cows but an occasional family had a goat or two. A South Dakota farmer lived right next to the Iowa border. Now this farmer understood all about borders but his billy goat didn't. One evening at milking time the goat was standing with its front feet in Iowa and its hind feet in South Dakota. In which state did the farmer milk his goat?

In the good old days, when you took the slop out of the hog trough you slopped the hogs. When you brought the horses the the tank after a day's work you watered the horses. When you put milk in the cat's dish—did you really milk the cat?

I'm sure that many of you that are my age or older had the chore of getting in the cobs to fuel the fire in the old kitchen range when mother was going to cook, can, bake, iron, or do the laundry. Our German mothers were shrewd women and would use the stick and carrot approach to get this unpleasant chore done. When mother had to do the laundry or ironing, it took so many cobs and the kitchen got so hot and we were so reluctant that mother had to use the stick approach.

However, when mother was going to bake she got many cobs quickly and willingly by dangling the carrot. Not once did she even have to mention those dirty little cobs waiting to be picked up in that filthy pig pen. We knew there would be bowls to be licked clean of the excess topping.

When you sit down at the table tonight, we won't put a label on you. You are here to enjoy a schmeckfest, a festival of tasting. Enjoy your food, enjoy your day, thank you for coming, and "lass es gut schmecken."

Folktales—Facts or Fiction?

Presented at the Twenty-second Annual Dakota History Conference, in Sioux Falls, South Dakota, May 31, 1990.

Folktales are rough retellings that aim at entertainment. Folktales are not children's stories—they are part of the literature of a whole people. They embody the history and mores of a culture, often illustrating the sanctions and restrictions of a given society. Just as stories of bravery, generosity, piety, and cleverness were told to promote these qualities, so too were violations of community and church laws and mores told to proscribe certain behaviors. Folklore is essentially an oral art, its form and detail slowly evolving through the years.

My grandparents subscribed to this theory, but my wife's grandfather enhanced it by suggesting, "Never but never let the truth stand between you and a good story!"

This cavalier attitude toward the truth disturbed me and in my mind reduced folktales to the level of fairy tales. But then my attitude was changed again by recent discoveries of pertinent old materials that have proven that in spite of embellishments, grandparents were very good at preserving their history with their stories. I have a new respect for oral history and renewed appreciation of folktales because after two-hundred years some of their stories are found to conform very closely to the known facts.

To show that there may be a modicum of validity in these old folktales, I will tell the story and then present some recent disclosures that lend credibility to the tale.

The first story is over two-hundred years old and concerns itself with the migration of my people from Germany to Russia. Because of a folktale, I photographed every rural cemetery that flashed by my bus window on a ride through those parts of Volhynia and Galicia where my ancestors stopped temporarily on their move from Germany to Russia.

My grandparents, who were not born till sixty years after the purported event, would tell of one of our men who became sick and died. When the Mennonites tried to bury the deceased in a local cemetery, the aroused natives exhumed the corpse and threw it over the fence. The hapless pilgrims appealed to the emperor for help. His highness dispatched some soldiers to see that a reburial was not interfered with, and sternly warned, "My subjects shall live in peace and they shall die in peace." Since all pioneer trails in all countries are marked by burial sites, it is easy to believe a man died. But is it believable that a small sect of religious heretics would have access to the King?

After my trip to the region I acquired a book, printed in Lemberg (now Lvov, Russia) in 1934. The title is *Mennonites in Kleinpolen 1784-1934* (Mennonites in Galicia 1784-1934). It records the oral tradition that soon after the arrival of the Mennonites, they had an unpleasant experience with a burial, when the first Mennonite death occurred on the 5th of March, 1787, and the deceased was to be buried. It was Johann Rupp, of Rosenberg, Number 8, forty-two years old. When the local peasants didn't want to let the corpse and funeral procession into the nearby Greek-Catholic cemetery, the Mennonites appealed to the political officials in Szczerec. They dispatched the military (the Hungarian cavalry), the cemetery was surrounded, the grave was dug, and the deceased was buried. As a result, a decree was soon issued (17 October 1787) by the Lemberg county authorities, advising the Evangelical congregations in Lemberg that the Catholic cemetery was open to all professing Christians. This happened at the express wish of Kaiser Joseph II, who asserted, "My subjects shall live with one another in peace, and likewise their dead shall lie in peace with one another."

True, the above story is admittedly based on oral tradition, but unlike my grandparents' story, it names the place (Rosenberg) it names people of record (Johann Rupp, ancestor of University of Kentucky basketball coach Adolph Rupp), it identifies the military unit (Hungarian Cavalry), it identifies the monarch (Joseph II), and at the end of the book, under a picture of Kaiser Joseph II, is a photo of a note of thanks written to him by his grateful Mennonite subjects.

Score one vote of confidence for the oral tradition.

In Russia, I was flabbergasted when I saw a wolf picture in an art gallery. Unable to read the title, I could not get a clue to what was happening; but I got the distinct feeling that this was a benign wolf manifesting kindness and gentleness, definitely not the savage beast I had been led to believe wolves are, especially Russian wolves. My grandmother had a long repertoire of Russian wolf stories; none of them had anything but fear and loathing for this villain.

Of her many stories I have chosen one that not only illustrates the modus operandi of these abominable killers, but also shows how a confrontation with them often brought out the worst traits in the frightened people they threatened. The Russian wolf stories are not peculiar to my Mennonite ancestors alone, but to all the Germans from Russia, and I suspect to many Russians as well. Prokofiev's *Peter and the Wolf* is one example that comes to mind.

The most dreaded sound in all of Russia, especially if you were traveling at night, was the howl of the wolf. The most dreaded of these was the distinctive call to the chase that was sent through the Russian night to summon the rest of the pack by the wolf that had come across the scent of the trail left by the intended victim. The passengers in the sled and the horses that pulled it recognized the call. Without any signal, the horses would break into a headlong run. They were urged on by the passengers in the sled.

After the initial call, there were answering calls from the right and the left. As more and more wolves joined the chase, the individual calls of the first wolves lost their identity in a full-throated chorus of menacing howls drawing ever closer. Terrifying as this was, it was even worse when the howling stopped, for now the wolves were close enough to close in for the kill, and this well-trained bunch of killers knew their parts in the unfolding drama well. There was no more need for verbal communication.

To the riders in the sled, the wolves were now fleeting shadows racing swiftly through the trees alongside the sled and on the road behind them. Everything in the sled was jettisoned to lighten the load for the horses. Sometimes young pigs would be taken along to throw to the wolves to gain a little time.

The wolves in the lead were not the first to attack. Those close behind the leaders charged first, at the hind legs of the horses to sever the hock strings. The forefeet of horses are formidable weapons if the horse can rise on its hind legs to use them. The wolves were well aware of this. With the hock disabled, the hind quarters of the horse went down, the lead wolves pulled down the front end of the horse by grabbing the throat or nose, and the rest of the pack then jumped in to finish the grisly job.

In another picture I saw, a wealthy nobleman and his servant were overtaken by the wolves. The servant suggested to his master that it was folly for both men to die and offered to jump from the sled and delay the wolves if the nobleman would agree to provide financial security for his wife and son. The nobleman agreed. The servant was killed, but his wife and child were cared for in a manner he never could have provided.

Some of the humans involved behaved shamefully under the stress. Like the woman in still another painting, they tossed their children to the wolves. In my grandmother's story the family waited too long before offering their baby. In their frenzy the wolves ran over the child. They had no idea that the tightly wrapped blanket contained a tender morsel. As soon as the inhabitants of a nearby village heard the wolves, the men armed themselves and raced to help. They arrived too late to save the people in the sled, but the infant was found alive and well in its blanket.

According to Willa Cather scholar Bernice Slote, this picture by Paul Powis (1887) may have inspired Willa Cather's wolf story in her novel *My Ántonia*. In that story the two

By Paul Powis (1887) Courtesy Nebraska State Historical Society.

Russian drivers threw the bride and groom to the wolves. In the book, *The White Lamb,* Mela Meisner Lindsay also has the story of wolves in pursuit of a bridal couple. In the mad dash for escape, the sled is upset and the young couple gets trapped under the overturned sled box. The horses are cruelly killed, but in the village, the ever-watchful hunters are alerted by the noise and get to the upset sled box before the wolves can get at their intended prey.

A paper about C. K. Howard at a previous Dakota History Conference gives an eyewitness account of a wolf kill in western South Dakota in 1891 as recorded by a guest of Mr. Howard:

The wolves would constantly circle around the horse, and one of the larger ones constantly snapped at the horse's head. Pretty soon the biggest of the wolves made a spring and grabbed ahold of the horse's hind legs above the joint and hung right on until he severed the tendons. The horse tried to kick but the mother wolf and younger wolves were circling around and kept him too busy. The moment the tendons of one leg were severed, the wolf let go of that one and ran on the other side and grabbed the horse by the other leg, just above the joint, and severed the cords or tendons on that side. The moment that was done the horse sank down on the ground, and then both of the big wolves jumped right for his middle and in an instant tore out his entrails. They did not wait for the horse to die; he was still struggling up on his front feet, but they began to consume him, attacking him from every side, and in an incredibly short time they completely gorged themselves . . . .

A picture in a *Smithsonian Magazine* shows the chase. The photographer reported that the moose escaped the wolf pack because the wolves could not get at his hind legs. The scene conforms in all aspects to the descriptions of the chase in the folktales. One question remains unanswered. There are those that insist there are no authenticated instances of wolves killing people. I suspect there are still Russians who believe they have killed and do kill. Cross breeding with dogs has produced a new strain, more cunning and vicious than even my grandmother could imagine.

My third story involves the 1874 crossing of my grandparents to America.

At some point in the difficult journey my great grandmother Goertz died. When I first heard of it from my grandfather, I believed the story implicitly. When in their retellings a sister and brother did not agree with each other or my grandfather on certain details, I became dubious of the entire episode. A search for the truth began.

A trip to the National Archives in Washington, D.C., for a copy of the ship's passenger list confirmed that Katherine Goertz, age thirty-five, did indeed die aboard ship on July 3, 1874, at 6:30 in the morning. The ship did not dock in New York till July 8, much too long to keep an unembalmed body in July.

The children were in general agreement that when death was imminent, the fellow travelers took the children and vacated the premise, leaving the distraught father alone with his dying wife. Presently the oldest child, John, was called to his mother's bedside. She admonished him and bade farewell. Each child in the order of their ages was summoned for their ritual. My grandfather was the third. The baby was a suckling, too young to respond. He was placed in the mother's arm. She kissed him, asked the father to take him, turned her head to the bulkhead, and died.

Now the women came in and bathed and dressed her and sewed her in sail cloth. My grandfather said a sack of coal was tied to her feet; his older sister said it was a steel plate. The weight at the feet was a humane gesture. These ships traveled so slowly that scavenger fish followed them to feed on the garbage thrown overboard. To the fish a human corpse was only so much garbage. The weight at the feet made the body sink from sight faster.

A plank with the body on it was balanced on the ship's rail. The ship's captain presided at the committal service. After the brief ceremony the plank was tilted and the deceased dropped into the ocean. My grandfather's last memory of his mother was of fish leaping out of the water and tearing at the shroud of the falling body.

It became important to me to find out if these ships were sailing vessels or steam powered. The second youngest son wrote the improbable account of his mother being sewn in silk. I rejected this theory at once, but I was concerned about sail cloth being available on a steamship.

I ordered a picture of the *Silesia* and found it to be a steam ship with sail assist. It answers the question about coal and sailcloth being available on the same ship. Another picture, of a burial at sea, was helpful. My attention was called to the picture in a German book by two young lady researchers. It was subsequently published in an American book on the occasion of the rededication of the Statue of Liberty in 1986 (*Liberty: The*

Statue and the American Dream, by Leslie Allen). After seeing
the picture and the ship's list, I'm inclined to accept my
grandfather's story of death and burial at sea at face value.

My fourth story might be called "The Mystery of Katherina." My wife's paternal grandfather was born, raised, and
married in this Russian village, Kotosufka. The first two or
three of his ten or eleven children were born there before the
move to Dakota Territory. All of my wife's aunts and uncles
agreed on all this except for the number of children there were
in the family. When the second youngest son, Uncle John, told
me three daughters were born in Russia, the other nine or ten
brothers and sisters insisted there were only two. Uncle John
was adamant. His parents had told him about her. The other
nine or ten had never heard of it from the parents, and there
was no record of a third child in the old family Bible.

Uncle John said her name was Katherina. When the family
left Russia, the mother was certain Katherina would not survive
the trip to America because she was a sickly child. On that
August day when the ship docked at Castle Garden in New

Kotosufka, Russia (1874), before leaving for America.

York, Katherina was still alive. The train took the group to the immigrant house by Moundridge, Kansas. Katherina survived the trip. In Kansas the Gerings found out that most of their close relatives had come to Dakota Territory. With fourteen other families, they made one more move, to Dakota.

When the locomotive, Black Hills No. 1, brought them to Yankton, Katherina was still alive. In this pioneer village on the Missouri, Grandpa bought a wagon and a team and a shovel and some other tools and started on the last leg of his trip to his relatives in East Freeman. The trail wasn't too hard to follow. In places it can still be seen in the spring of the year before the grass gets tall. It was on this last stretch of road where the trail crossed the Jim River that little Katherina died. She was so close to the end of the trail that she was taken the rest of the way.

That night as the rest of the weary group made their beds under their wagons or under the stars, Grandpa Gering took his new shovel and turned the first sod on the land he would file on. There was no wood for a coffin. Katherina was buried in her little blanket.

The surviving members of the family assured me that Uncle John had fabricated the story.

On our trip to the archives in Washington we found Grandpa Gering and his family on the ship's passenger list. There were three children. The baby's name was Katherina. I would have liked to tell Uncle John, but he had passed on. Uncle John's veracity was vindicated one more time.

In 1980 my wife's mother moved to a retirement apartment. My daughters came to help clean up the old home. In the ceiling of an upstairs bedroom was a small trapdoor. One of my daughters got a step ladder and flashlight to see if anything was beyond the door. There was a paper package covered with the dust of the ages. In the package was a tattered, old German Bible. I looked at the fly leaf—printed in New York—obviously not brought from Russia. I thumbed through the brittle pages and came upon two folded sheets that had been removed from an older Bible and tucked away here for safe keeping. The first of the sheets was a record of births. The third entry reads, "In the year 1873 on the 5th of October, a daughter was born to me. Name, Katherina." I was so elated with this discovery that I didn't even think it strange that he should say the child was born to him. After all, isn't this the kind of talk you would expect from one who had said, "Never but never let the truth stand between you and a good story!" The second sheet, titled "Deaths," has this entry, "In the year 1874, on October 16, Katherina was taken up to her sacred rest."

To Uncle John I offer gratitude for keeping a story alive till it could be proven true.

The alpha of this next tale is in south Russia, the omega in South Dakota. It concerns a gentleman and his love of dogs. His name was Jacob Graber, but he is remembered as Poltawitz because of the Russian town of Poltava. Historians remember Poltava as the place where Peter the Great defeated Charles XII and his Swedish army. My people in Freeman think of Poltava as the place where this man was chief warden of a wealthy nobleman's forests and lakes. Hence his nickname, Poltawitz.

When some of his many descendants wanted copies of his picture, it was taken to a photo studio. At that time it was a dirty picture of a man and his dog, his gun and his game. The photographer decided to clean the picture before he copied it. As he cleaned, Grandma slowly emerged from the grime the old scoundrel had applied to obliterate her. Evidently he only wanted a framed picture of a macho man and his dog. To this day Grandma continues to peer out from behind the curtain on the original; the dog has completely faded from the scene. And in the picture, Poltawitz has a normal human ear. In a family picture about the same time, Poltawitz's ear looks like a typical man's ear. But in a photo taken fifty years later, in which the children's spouses had almost doubled the size of the family, the ear seems smaller. Indeed, it is smaller and thereby hangs the tale.

Poltawitz had not been in America very long when he started accumulating dogs as he had in Russia. If a man's wealth would have been measured by dogs, Poltawitz would have been considered a rich man. Mrs. Poltawitz did not appreciate his idea of wealth and delivered an ultimatum: either dogs go or she goes. She insisted the issue was not negotiable but finally did agree to one dog.

One by one the dogs were disposed of until there were only two left. Since both dogs seemed equal in those dog attributes Poltawitz admired, the elimination process now became exceedingly difficult. When the solution presented itself, it was a masterpiece of simplicity. He put one of the family cats in the sack, took his gun, summoned his two dogs and walked into the middle of the prairie that had not yet been turned by the plow. He reasoned that when he released the cat, it would be caught by the dog with the best hunting instinct, and that is the dog he would keep.

Now it so happened that the cat Poltawitz had put in the sack was no featherweight feline finagler. This cat was the turn-of-the-century Garfield. As soon as the cat was let out of the sack, it sized up the situation and found a place of refuge the wily old man had overlooked. In a very brief instant she climbed Poltawitz's back and perched on the top of his head. For an old man he had some agile gyrations. Was it the dog's fault that when he lunged he got a mouthful of his master's ear instead of cat? Needless to say, this was not the dog that survived the selection process.

You ask me, do I believe this story? I invite you to listen to the second paragraph in a column from the 9 September 1975 *Yankton Press and Dakotan:* "Clarence Gosch has the misfortune of losing part of his ear. They had fed the dog when Clarence stepped out doors and the dog snapped at his ear and took part of it off."

Those tales in the "Tall Tales" department are obviously told for entertainment, but many of them have real value because they reveal aspects of history that might otherwise be forgotten. Since Freeman was abandoned by the railroad, the ground around the former track bed has been altered considerably and our young people have no idea that much of the rail right-of-way went through some swampy lowland.

One gentleman who owned property adjacent to the railroad was much annoyed when many people assumed this worthless land didn't belong to anyone and started dumping their junk and refuse in the potholes. The irate landowner consulted a lawyer, who told him to put up a sign advising people that anyone disposing of garbage on this property would be prosecuted and fined. He was greatly disturbed that the sign he put up aggravated the problem. The growth of the junk pile was now quickly accelerated. The rapid growth of the pile of refuse was awesome. Again he appealed to his legal counsel. The lawyer went to see. Indeed there was a sign. It was large. It bore the legend "FINE FOR DUMPING."

This of course is an indicator of the language problems suffered by these Germans from Russia. Every family, every group, every town had its favorite language problem stories. Some of the best ones defy translation and will soon be forgotten. Some that depend on one key word can be told in mixed audiences (mixed in this instance meaning German- and English-speaking). This next story is cheerfully told by the Volga Germans in Lincoln, Nebraska.

In Nebraska as in South Dakota, the German-from-Russia sodbusters did their plowing with walking plows. They couldn't wait to get prosperous enough to get a riding plow. One Volga German found to his dismay that progressive farming wasn't necessarily better. The long hours of jostling about on a hard iron seat produced a boil of astounding size and excruciating pain. Now he couldn't ride and could hardly walk. He was taken to Lincoln to buy a cushion for the plow seat. It is important that you know the German word for cushion and pillow is the same—*Kissen*. The saleslady knew no German, the suffering German knew no English. When she asked him what he wanted he answered, "*Kissen*."

Impishly she put her fingers on her lips and asked, "Here kissen?"

Angrily he put his finger on the afflicted part and answered, "*Nein! Nein! Hier Kissen!*"

Not only were the Germans frustrated in their attempts to put their German thoughts into English; they were thoroughly baffled by the English idioms. Here is another example:

Very few know that at one time Freeman legally had a pool hall. Later a city ordinance made it illegal to play pool or dance in Freeman. I do not know if the law was ever repealed, but enthusiastic dancers and pool players now pursue their favorite recreation without harassment. It was not always so.

When the elders of my church found out that my grandfather was "shooting pool," they convened a special church meeting to deal with this violation of church ethics. The preacher that would read the charges was confronted with translating "shooting pool" into German. This is what my grandfather and the assembly heard: "*Es ist uns gessagt worden das der Sep Schrag tut Bull Schiessen.*" "It has been brought to our attention that Joseph Schrag engages in shooting the bull."

"Folktales . . . embody the history and mores of a culture" is a line from our opening statement. Some tales describe an attitude toward a new challenge more vividly than a scholarly dissertation. When such stories describe an emotion (fear, anger, love) or use humor to help us remember an incident, attention to detail becomes a lesser concern. The era of the "huggy buggy" ride is best remembered by stories generated by participants and embellished by delighted onlookers.

When the car pushed the horse and buggy out of use and memory, stories of buggy courtship were replaced by new stories, poems, and songs about romance in the flivver. The flavor of the era is best captured and retained in limericks, parodies, and light humor. To this day cartoonists respond so quickly to the beginnings of cultural change that it is difficult to determine if they observe or instigate.

Impressing the girls.

Imagine the sorry plight of young men whose parents couldn't afford a car. These young cousins believed only ten commandments were recorded because the eleventh commandment was so obvious it didn't need to be committed to writing. Everybody knows all is fair in love and war. In that spirit these men, who had only a buggy, rigged up this contraption with it. They would send pictures of this to girls at a distance who didn't know they didn't have a car, girls who didn't know that removing the shafts from a buggy didn't automatically turn it into a horseless carriage. Girls who didn't know that empty syrup cans wedged between the spring leaves had nothing to do with illumination and a sprocket wheel salvaged from the junk pile didn't steer this carriage.

One of these gentlemen found such a lady in Chasley, North Dakota, where they still live happily married after all of these years.

It didn't take young men long to discover that the ratio of success in the pursuit of romantic interests was in direct proportion to the quality of the car you were driving. The better your car, the better your chance of getting the girl. When the young man called for the young lady all alone in the family car, both sets of parents worried. The father of the boy worried about the car, the mother of the girl worried about her daughter's virtue. This concern is succinctly spelled out in a story of that time.

A young lady was surprised when her mother denied a request to go to a house party in the community. The refusal was unexpected. Heretofore the mother had always granted permission. The girl wanted to know why the rules had been changed. The mother explained:

"I have heard about these parties and I don't like what has been happening lately. A fellow will come up to you and ask, 'Would you like a cold lemonade?'

Then you will answer, 'I don't mind.'

Then he will say, 'I've got my father's car tonight. Would you like to go for a ride?'

Again you will answer, 'I don't mind.'

He will drive you out on some deserted road and stop the car and put his arm around you, and that's when I start worrying."

Then as now, the daughter eventually had her way and went to the party. In the early hours of the morning, a sleepless mother heard the sound of a car chugging up the driveway, she heard the car door slam and running feet kicking the gravel on the path. She heard the front door open and close and then an exuberant daughter was at her bedside.

"Oh mother," the girl chortled, "It was just like you said it would be and it was wonderful! Johnny was there and he came up to me and asked if I would like a glass of cold lemonade. I told him I wouldn't mind. After he got the lemonade he said he had his father's car and asked if I would like to go for a ride. I told him I wouldn't mind. So he drove down a deserted country road and he turned off the engine, and then mother you would have been so proud of me. It was then I remembered what you had told me, and before he could put his arm around me, I put my arm around him and I told him, 'Now let your mama do the worrying!'"

Parents were not the only concerned people involved in the car-induced revolution in courtship. The man who owned that remote plot of land at the end of that deserted road dubbed "Lover's Lane" had a real concern too. One such concerned citizen used bold letters to put his concern on the gate:

SHUT THE GATE LOVER BOY. OUR HEIFER IS A LOT HARDER TO CATCH THAN THE ONE YOU'RE CHASING.

These tales about courtship in cars, embellished or not, true or not, have preserved the essence of cultural conflicts in changing periods of our history. Not only do they make historical events memorable, they make history fun. I am in total accord with Washington Irving, who wrote, "I am always of easy faith in such matters, and am ever willing to be deceived where deceit is pleasant and costs nothing. I am therefore a ready believer in relics, legends and local anecdotes of goblins and great men; and would advise all travellers who travel for their gratification to be the same. What is it to us whether these stories be true or false, so long as we can persuade ourselves into the belief of them, and enjoy all the charm of reality?"

Chapel Talk

This chapel talk was given at Freeman Junior College, October 30, 1990.

In 1873 the railroad came to Yankton. If you lived in Yankton at that time, you already made it a point to meet the train when it pulled in at the depot because you were assured of seeing something different and strange getting off the train almost every time.

In the middle of March, the train watchers saw a well-known general and his troops get off the train. It was the flamboyant General George Armstrong Custer and his 7th Cavalry on their way to their ultimate death at the battle of Little Big Horn. Excitement ran high in Yankton. Young men rushed to enlist. A young Yankton musician joined and became Custer's bandmaster.

In the excitement no one remembered or cared that General George Armstrong Custer was of Mennonite stock. I read one sentence from the book *General George A. Custer: My Life on the Plains,* by Milo Milton Quaife. "In 1684 Paul Custer migrated from the German Rhineland to Pennsylvania as one of a company of Mennonites who constituted the second band of immigrants to settle in William Penn's new colony." So the Custer family had been around for a long time and they had been Mennonite.

When, a short time later that same year, the real Mennonites stepped off the Yankton train, it is unlikely that the train watchers guessed that these strange people still lived the lifestyle and practiced the same religion that the famous general's ancestors did when they first set foot on American soil.

One of the things that set the general apart from these German-Russian Mennonites was the matter of humility. The

general aspired for the presidency of the country. The Mennonites aspired for only 160 acres of this state. The general longed
for glory and publicity. The Mennonites wanted obscurity. The
general wanted the acclaim of the masses. The Mennonites
wanted seclusion.

Like the other groups of Germans from Russia, the
Mennonites wanted to settle in one area, in one solid group.
This could not be done by Yankton because earlier settlers had
put down their claim stakes at various locations. There was still
room for the Mennonites, but the available claims were
scattered, and it was impossible to settle in one contiguous
settlement. If they settled by Yankton they would have to
contend with an occasional Scandinavian in their midst, or an
Irishman, or a Dutchman, or a Bohemian.

But up north, here in Hutchinson and Turner Counties,
large areas of unclaimed land were available. All the Germans
from Russia came to this area. The Wittenberg people settled
by Olivet, the Katschup by Tripp and Parkston, the Heilbronner, Johannestahlers, Kasslers and Klein Kasslers from
Menno to Freeman. The Hutterites settled along the James
River from Olivet to Emery in the north and east to the vicinity
of Silver Lake. There the Low-German community started and
extended through Dolton and Marion to the Brotherfield church
north of Parker. The Swiss occupied an area approximately
fifteen miles long by fifteen miles wide, east of Freeman. None
of the new settlers strayed far from their ethnic and religious
enclaves.

The neighboring Germans from Russia that were Reformed and Lutheran presented no problem for the three
Mennonite groups. They could be avoided and they were. The
big concern for the Mennonites was how to cope with their
fellow Mennonites from the other two groups.

By far the largest of the three groups was the Low-
German settlement. What were they to do with the Hutterites
and Swiss?

The Hutterites were still trying to decide if it is better to live in a colony or establish themselves on a claim of their own. Some Hutterites were leaving the colonies and joining with the other "Prairie Leut" in private ownership of land or moving to town. A case in point would be Dr. A. A. Wipf. He left the colony and set up a very successful practice in Freeman.

On the other hand there were those who divested themselves of their property and returned to the colony. A case in point would be two of the three men who sold their land to the railroad for the Freeman townsite. Mr. Mendel writes in his *History of Freeman,* "Until the fall of 1879, all you could see on the present site of Freeman were three sod houses belonging to Fred Waldner, Mike Tschetter, and David Kleinsasser." Mr. Mendel goes on to say that after these men sold their land to the railroad company, Fred Waldner and Mike Tschetter joined the Bon Homme Colony.

As a point of interest, the aforementioned Dr. A. A. Wipf told of Freeman getting its name from this incident. When the railroad representative gave these three men their checks for their land, one of them looked at his check and considered what an incredible amount of money it was, and how he could pay the many outstanding bills he had, and exclaimed, "*Jezt bin ich ein freier Mann.*"

The railroad man asked the interpreter, "What did he say?"

The interpreter answered, "He said, 'Now I am a free man'."

The railroad man said, "What an appropriate name for this new town."

The Swiss were another matter. They were just making a change in their religious orientation from Amish to General Conference—from ultra conservative to ultra liberal. It was confusing to the larger Mennonite community but most confusing to the Swiss themselves. Even in my youth they held many church meetings to reach some sort of an agreement on what would be acceptable and what was sinful.

As long as each of the three Mennonite groups stayed in their own area, the other two groups were not too much concerned about their doctrinal differences. But when some of the young people started to intermarry and one of the newly-weds went to the spouse's church, the differences became a big concern.

I wish I knew, but I had no idea how the congregation reacted when my Low-German grandfather Goertz and his older brother married Swiss sisters by the name of Graber, and a younger brother married a Schrag girl, also Swiss.

How did the Hutterites react when a young Mr. Hofer married a Pankratz girl who was obviously Low German?

Unfortunately, these people did not pass on the many morsels of gossip and consternation that were bandied about. I did hear of one instance where a boy from one group married a girl from another group and brought her to his church. There was outrage. They were told that she was not acceptable until she was retrained in her religious thinking and was rebaptized. Furthermore, if she did not consent to do this, he also would no longer be welcome in his church. In this instance, the young couple left their churches and joined a church in another denomination.

Others succumbed to the demands of the church they would eventually join—in most instances the man's church, but not always. In the case of my Low-German grandfather—he joined grandma's church, and as a consequence I have a Low-German name, speak the Swiss dialect, go to the North Church, and spent many of my seventy-two years trying to figure out who I am.

There was concern. There must be a better way. The ministers of the Hutterites and Low Germans and the Swiss held joint meetings to decide if their doctrines were not compatible enough to accept young married people from another church into their congregation. It was decided a church letter would be acceptable in most cases. Some churches that were willing to accept the doctrines you had been taught still insisted you be rebaptized if you had not been baptized by immersion. If you had been immersed it was important if you had been immersed forward or backward. A big step had been taken toward ecumenical co-existence by the three groups. In retrospect, many old timers feel the most significant unifying event was the building of this school. Some think the Schmeck-fest is the finest example of the three groups working together and obviously enjoying it.

One would assume when agreement was reached by the ministers how to handle the memberships of outsiders that married into their church, the problem was laid to rest. As the song in *Porgy and Bess* says, "It ain't necessarily so."

You ask, what else could go wrong?

To show you, let me tell of an incident that happened in the Swiss community before there were two churches. This was told to me by the man involved.

In the pioneering days, young people regularly had Sunday afternoon parties. They would decide at church at whose home they would meet on that day. My mother would tell how after dinner she and her brothers and sisters (nine of them) would start walking to the appointed place. As they passed the neighboring farms, those young people would join the group. By the time the party site was reached they had a sizeable assembly.

Everybody walked. The parents told them the horses must rest on Sunday and young people should too. If the kids didn't have sense enough to stay home and get some much needed rest, they could go party but the horses stayed at home. All parents were of the same opinion: all horses rested, all young people walked.

The grandfather that told me his story lived on the fringes of the Swiss community. If the party was at the other side of the area it was a long, long walk to the party. It was much closer to his Norwegian neighbors so he would go there. Like the Mennonites, they too partied on Sunday afternoon. They also walked. It was much like the Mennonite parties except they talked Norwegian and they danced.

So my informant danced.

Some one heard of it and reported him to the church elders. Church discipline was awesome. He had to appear before the congregation, confess his sins, apologize to the membership, and promise to sin no more. This he knew beforehand was the penalty for getting caught. But he thought it was highly unfair when the minister counted three transgressions on the one incident. (1) The accused brother danced. (2) And even more despicable, the accused brother danced on Sunday. (3) And most loathsome of all, he danced with Norwegian girls. The old gentleman told me he repented and apologized, eventually married a proper Schweitzer girl, and died in good standing in his church.

Not so with some of his friends. I don't know if they danced with Norwegian girls but they married them. Others married non-Mennonite school teachers. The old ministers in their previous discussions had not anticipated this. Since these newcomers were non-Mennonites and did not involve the other Mennonite churches, the ministerium did not get officially involved. Each congregation handled this problem in their own way.

One would think that once attitudes about accepting new members from other denominations had been adjusted and rules relaxed everything would be smooth sailing. Well not quite. Now there were a few that wanted to marry divorced spouses. And in this day and age we ponder the question of membership for homosexuals. There are always problems.

When the Norwegians and other non-traditional Mennonites were accepted into the congregations, the people found out to their surprise that these were wonderful people; they were just as nice as the rest of us. But as you may have already guessed, in spite of their good nature and industry and piety—there was now another problem!

Do you care to guess what it was?

Though the new members came to church faithfully, it was quite meaningless for them. They didn't understand the German sermons or songs. The more the congregation got to know and appreciate these newcomers, the more they wanted to accommodate them. In their effort some did the unthinkable. They started to tamper with one of the solid footings of the Anabaptist religion. They started to talk about changing the services from German to English. My grandmother and her peers that made the move from Russia could not believe my father's generation was serious when they suggested a language change. My grandmother talked to God in German, his word was written in German, and she was not ready to change this sacred arrangement.

The subject generated much heat but it also had many humorous incidents. Since you already know the ultimate outcome of this issue, and hardly any of you know German any more, I'll not pursue the story of the language issue, but I would like to make an observation on its outcome.

Two years ago the *Mennonite Weekly Review* noted that the non-ethnic Mennonites, that is, those Mennonites who are not of Germanic stock, exceed in numbers those of us who stem from the old stock. I wasn't there, but I am told the World Conference in Winnipeg was a kaleidoscope of color of the different races and a babble of different languages and some of the participants in the programs even danced.

In the Freeman area a minister with the Scandinavian name of Peterson now preaches in one of our Mennonite churches and another man with an English name, Hatheway, guides your Mennonite religious studies.

The story of the man that got caught dancing with the Norwegian girls now only shows the suspicion with which "outsiders" were viewed, it also gives an inkling of the strict discipline the churches used to keep their members in line. Everything from violations of dress codes, to unacceptable social conduct, to deviations from prescribed doctrinal code was ruled on by the elders and congregation. Retribution was sure and severe. Most transgressors publicly repented and apologized. Some did not.

Those that did not feel their conduct was wrong, and would not apologize, were banned. They left the church and in most instances the community. If the group of accused sinners was large enough, they left the church and started their own church. There is one instance in the community where the disagreeing factions could agree on only one thing. They agreed to meet by the church on an appointed day with their saws and saw the church in half.

The stories about church discipline are legion. My time, however, is up.

As you listen to Jan Gleysteen, listen carefully for those things that speak to us of language, baptism, church discipline, and isolation. *"Sondert euch ab (von der Weld), spricht der Herr"* (2 Corinthians, 6:17).

These were tools designed to keep the Mennonites together and pure. Improperly used, they become divisive and destructive. That is why history is important. We can always learn from it.

From Missionary to Mummy: A South Dakotan Comes Home

This paper was presented at the Twenty-fourth Annual Dakota History Conference in Sioux Falls, South Dakota, May 28, 1992.

Burials in South Dakota have traditionally been somber and simple rituals. Some of the aboriginal inhabitants honored their dead with large burial mounds.

But the settlers from Europe tended to bury their dead in a simple box in a shallow grave without any show of ostentation.

The wooden marker burned in the next prairie fire and the mound of dirt over the corpse slowly settled until only a grassy depression on the treeless plain remained. There was neither time nor the where-with-all for pomp at the funeral or a grand and stately tombstone to mark the site.

Of course, as with almost everything else, there were exceptions to the rule. Some exceptions were by design, others were caused by bizarre happenings of chance. One of each sort happened in my community within three years of each other.

In 1927, a certain citizen, seemingly preoccupied with a burial place that would preserve the remembrance of his life, built a concrete monstrosity, at a cost of $10,000. If you think the high cost of leaving is a modern phenomenon, think of the true value of $10,000 in 1927. A road was platted to the tomb but was never made.

A bronze memorial plaque was made and mounted. A decorative wrought iron fence decorates the top. The arch over the middle accommodates two immense steel vault doors. The thick walls go into the ground seven feet and are anchored in place by concrete corner posts, reinforced with steel angle irons on the outside corners. Not only are the heavy vault doors kept closed with combination vault locks, a four inch steel bar is in place to thwart unauthorized entry.

If getting in is difficult, it is extremely easy to get out—if you can get out of the grave. The top of the structure is wide open. In 1929, two years after it was finished, the man who had this roofless mausoleum built made certain that his would be the first body interred here with a well directed gun shot to his body.

Meanwhile, in northern China, a man and his wife were contemplating a visit to their South Dakota home. Jonathan Schrag was born in 1875, one year after his parents came to America from Russia, making him one of the first babies born in my group of German immigrants from Russia. In due time he also became the first missionary from my church. After twenty-one years in China he was coming home for this second furlough. To fulfill a life-long desire to visit the Holy Land he routed his trip to South Dakota through India and the Holy Land. Little did he realize what the consequences of this decision would be.

February 6, 1930, Rev. and Mrs. Schrag sailed from Shanghai; April 6 they arrived in Jerusalem. Rev. Schrag was not feeling well. Mrs. Schrag jokingly asked him, "Are we going to have to bury you in Jerusalem?" He thought it was a bad joke. Five days later, April 11, 1930, Jonathan was dead.

When the cablegram arrived with the message, "Jonathan dead," the shocked family in South Dakota sent a cablegram back with the terse message, "Bring body home." By the time the body did get home, the family found out that international travel for a corpse is governed by rules much more stringent than those applied to living travelers.

It took a month and three days to prepare the body to comply with the legal requirements for international transport. The remains finally left Jerusalem on May 15 and arrived in Marion Junction on June 14. The family was first led to believe the body would come on Monday and set the funeral for the following Sunday in case there was a delay. This was a fortuitous bit of foresight.

The family and two funeral home directors were on constant alert. The reason for two directors was the involvement of two caskets. One hearse was required for the shipping box on the train, another with a new casket into which the deceased would be transferred for showing and burial. The first days of waiting were in vain, and then a telegram arrived in time to be published in the *Marion Record* that Mr. Schrag would arrive Saturday morning. Again the family and morticians assembled at the depot and again disappointment, again no Mr. Schrag. He did finally arrive on the late afternoon train. Since the family had ample time to prepare for the funeral they assumed every detail had been attended to. To their amazement there were still many unexpected obstacles to overcome.

When young nephews, strong and muscular farm boys, tried to lift the box from the baggage car they almost dropped it. The shipping weight was 850 pounds. Once the box was gotten on the ground they were confronted with another dilemma. They couldn't open the box to transfer the body to its American coffin.

Many of the following facts were furnished by Esmond Wilson, funeral director in Parker, at that time, whose funeral car conveyed the body to the grave, and who acted as an assistant to the funeral director in charge, Benjamin Yopp, of Marion. Mr. Wilson published the information in a mortician's magazine named *Casket and Sunnyside*.

The outer box was made of oak one-and-one-half inches thick. There were three hoops of bar iron, three eights of an inch thick and two inches wide, with a bar bolted across the top. The bolts had been riveted; they could not be turned with wrenches and metal cutting tools had to be sent for. The screws that held the oak lid down also resisted screw drivers and it seemed to take an eternity to get the box open. Once the oak lid was removed a metal box was revealed. More painstaking work and this barrier was breached only to reveal another metal box. When this top was finally chiseled off it seemed the box was filled with sawdust. To keep the body from tossing about in the box during turbulent weather it had been packed in sawdust. After removing oak and zinc and lead, the matter of the sawdust should have been easily resolved. It was, but its removal uncovered the biggest shock of the entire event. Mr. Wilson's account in *Casket and Sunnyside* continues: "It (the body) was wrapped like a Egyptian mummy. The eye sockets were empty, no eyeballs at all; mouth partly open, the face being only part exposed to view. The face was jet black and glistened like a shoe."

The Jerusalem undertaker must have lied through his teeth when he filled out and signed the paper that accompanied the box. As you will see, the "Undertaker" in the case did not function to any great extent, being more an inspector than embalmer or funeral director. His statement follows:

"This is to certify that I, Elias Thos. Gelat, undertaker, have seen the body of Mr. Jonathan J. Schrag, an American citizen of Marion, South Dakota, who died at the German Deaconess Hospital, Jerusalem, placed (the body) after embalming into a lead air-tight shell, enclosed in a zinc lined strong coffin, hooped with iron.

"I have identified the body as placed in those chests, with the likeness of Mr. Jonathan J. Schrag on his passport, and certify that nothing else has been placed inside."

The relatives insist there wasn't any resemblance between the body in the box and the passport picture. According to *Casket and Sunnyside,* "At the close of the funeral service, it was announced that those who wished to view the remains might do so. If any were there who hesitated, they should rather refrain from doing so because he did not look natural at all." As it turned out the undertaker didn't even embalm the body.

Among the official papers accompanying the body to this country was one from the American Vice Consul at Jerusalem, conveying two statements from Dr. Tanfik Cannan, hospital physician; one concerning the death of Jonathan Schrag and one describing the method of embalming as done by himself. In America many think it is unethical for a physician to own his own drug dispensary. How would you like to entrust your high risk surgery to a man who is also the undertaker if his medical ministrations fail?

Dr. Tanfik Cannan, physician in charge.

"I, Dr. Tanfik Cannan, physician of the German Deaconess Hospital, Jerusalem, do hereby certify that on the 8th day of April, 1930, Mr. Jonathan J. Schrag, an American citizen of Marion, South Dakota, and born therein, aged 54 years, was brought to the German Hospital for treatment. He suffered from sub-acute suppurating otitis media which has caused a cerebral abscess and general cerebro-spinal meningitis.

The other paper reads as follows:

Dr. Tanfik, mortician in charge.

"I, the undersigned, Dr. Tanfik Cannan, Physician of the Deaconess Hospital, Jerusalem, declare having embalmed the body of Mr. Jonathan Schrag, an American citizen aged fifty-four years, who died of otitis media and cerebro-spinal meningitis at the said hospital at 2 P.M. on the 11th day of April 1930, in the following manner:

"The circulatory system was injected through several arteries with five litres of a 20 percent solution of sodium arsenate (containing also 500 C C M of formaline).

"After 24 hours the three cavities were completely eviscerated and the body was submerged for 48 hours in 95 percent alcohol with formaline."

From this we may presume the pious parson was probably properly pickled for preservation.

"The cavities were allowed to dry for forty-eight hours and then were filled with pure zinc sulphate crystals and sutured. The whole skin was varnished repeatedly with venise alcohol varnish.

"The whole body was wrapped with thick layers of bandages moistened in a concentrated solution of zinc sulphate, and zinc sulphate crystals were thickly strewed between and over these layers of bandages.

"The body of Mr. Jonathan Schrag treated and after death embalmed by me, was placed in a lead coffin, surrounded with an antiseptic mixture as subscribed in the Public Health Ordinance No. 2. The lead shell was then well soldered, as well as the zinc coffin which lined the wood chest which was closed with screws and encircled with three iron hoops, tightly screwed and riveted. This container was so constructed and sealed as to prevent the issuance of any liquid therefrom. Then the seals of the Public Health Department and the American Consulate General at Jerusalem were affixed on the body of the chest and lid.

"Exclusion made all danger of infection and considering the satisfaction sanitary condition in our City, there would be no objection to the transportation of the mortuary remains to the United States.

"In witness whereof I have here-unto set my hand on the 24th day of April, 1930, at Jerusalem, Palestine."

After the initial shock the family and morticians had a conference by the railroad tracks and decided to leave Mr. Schrag in his lead, zinc, and oak coffins. The body would be taken to his brother's home five miles east of Freeman where it would lie in state till the funeral on the following day. Even at the home the combined weight of the three coffins posed a problem. Not enough men could squeeze through the door of the house with the heavy box to carry it in. Planks and rollers were procured and Mr. Schrag was rolled up the steps and into the house.

When an inordinately large number of cars started to assemble at the church, a man with a box camera climbed the windmill on the farm across the road from the church to capture the moment for posterity. His endeavor was premature. There were many more cars to come. *Casket and Sunnyside* gives the following account:

Jonathan Schrag funeral at the Salem-Zion Mennonite Church in 1930.

"The funeral was the largest ever held in that part of South Dakota, over 5,000 people being present in 1,100 automobiles. The services were held in the Salem-Zion Mennonite Church, nine miles from Marion, on Sunday afternoon, June 15. Mr. Schrag was a very prominent Mennonite and was known among the people of that sect in all parts of the world; hence the size of his funeral. Seven ministers officiated in the services, two of them English and five speaking in the native tongue, German. Forty-one automobiles carried the family and relatives from the home to the church, following the brief service at the home."

Not only was the family large, it was and still is a very musical family. Special music was provided between the sermons by nieces and nephews.

Casket and Sunnyside continues: "The capacity of the church was 1,800, the balance of those in attendance being seated in the basement and on the church lawns. Amplifiers were brought into use so that all present were able to hear the sermons which lasted from 1 to 4:40 o'clock.

"At the close of the service in the church the casket was opened and for an hour friends and acquaintances passed in order viewing the body. Then followed the committal service at the grave, consuming another hour."

The remainder of the article in *Casket and Sunnyside* is devoted to plaudits for the morticians and their trade. The final paragraph raises questions about the lasting quality of Egyptian embalming compared to American methods:

"In connection, one question of importance arises. Even in the dry soil of South Dakota, how will the body of Mr. Schrag, submitted to the methods of Egyptian embalming (and that is what was done) stand up as compared with a body embalmed after the present-day method? How will that body look after ten years?" —*Casket and Sunnyside.*

I am confident that Mr. Schrag and his relatives couldn't care less how the body looked after ten years or even now after sixty-two years. Only Jonathan Schrag's name and a brief reference to his death in Jerusalem on his tombstone distinguish his grave from those of his relatives, neighbors, and friends.

With the exception of the immediate family, not many people, even in my community, realize that in one of these graves a mummy reposes. The long and costly preparation for the burial will soon be entirely forgotten. It doesn't seem important in my home town. The attitude is unlike that of a long-departed Bostonian.

In Boston's north end is "Copp's Hill Burying Ground." A woman, striving for immortality, prepared for her death and urged others to prepare as she did, by designing her own tombstone and ordering the following epitaph engraved on it:

"Stop here my friends and cast an eye,
As you are now, so once was I;
As I am now, so you must be,
Prepare for death and follow me."

An irreverent wag with chalk added two more lines and reflect my sentiments:

"To follow you I'm not content
Unless I know which way you went."

My Sullied Saints: Things I Did Not Learn in Catechism

The author presented this as a luncheon address at the Germans from Russia Heritage Society Convention in Fargo, North Dakota, July 8-11, 1993. The text has been transcribed from tape by Armand Bauer.

Those of you who have never had the opportunity to stand behind a podium before a large audience, I want to assure that it is a great honor. And, yes, it is terrifying, too, especially when the road up to it is strewn with pitfalls. My good friend Professor Marzolf had asked me over a year ago whether I would talk to the group at the convention about the Hutterites and Mennonites and the differences between them—how one can tell the difference between them. Since I had such a talk prepared, I agreed to do this. But this spring I got a letter from a certain Victor Knell in North Dakota informing me that he was co-chairman of this convention and instead of the talk I was prepared to give, to give a talk that was "light." This I considered an affront, for I now felt that the Mennonites were being equated to beer and that I could have a choice of making it "lite" or "regular." I wrote to both gentlemen protesting that the subject that was assigned to me was not "light." Mr. Knell replied in a very convincing letter—note, however, that Professor Marzolf walks with the big stick, but Mr. Knell writes as the voice of authority—saying that "surely there must have been times when the Mennonites and Hutterites used humor, even the proverbs and folk tales used by them to teach their children and to make a point with some kind of wit." And of course, Victor was right. But Victor also made it very clear in that letter (by other things he said) that he had never read a novel by James Michener, because James Michener in his novel *Centennial* devotes a little space to writing about the Mennonites. I am sure that if there had been German-Russians in Pennsylvania, he would have included a reference to them as well, instead of just to the Mennonites.

For your information I want to read just three short paragraphs from *Centennial.* "In most other parts of the world, the Mennonites would have seemed impossibly rigid, but when compared to the Amish (in Pennsylvania) they were downright frivolous. For they indulged in mildly worldly pleasure, were expert in conducting business, and allowed their children other choices in farming." Expert in conducting business is correct. And I know your ancestors as well as I know my own.

My father was in business on the main street of Freeman, and your people drove as hard a bargain as any Mennonite I knew. Some Mennonite children even went to school, but when they did farm they did it with vigor and with wonderful skill in extracting from the soil its maximum yield. When this was accomplished they became uncanny in their ability to peddle it for its maximum profit. Mennonite women in particular were gifted in selling. They knew to the penny what they could demand from a customer, giving him in turn such a bargain that he was likely to come back. And I've known a lot of you who are not Mennonite, and your women too have conducted bake sales and provided the food for the auction sales who have the uncanny ability to raise money. It makes me sort of bristle when the Scots are said to be thrifty, also referred to as being canny, while the Yankees are shrewd, and even you German-Russians are considered quite sparing and prudent in your business deals. But, then, the Mennonites are accused of being downright *geizig* (stingy). The merchants in Yankton and Sioux Falls shudder when they see a Mennonite coming in the place, and they start laughing and say, "Here come the Mennonites with a ten-dollar bill in one hand and the ten commandments in the other, and a firm resolve in their hearts not to break either."

I want to read another paragraph from Michener's *Centennial*—I won't read all of it. If you can just substitute your family name for "Mennonite," you will see how hard it is to tell the difference between you and me, and consequently the stories that are strictly and truly of Mennonite origin. Michener goes on, "The Mennonites of Lancaster County (Pennsylvania) were a lusty lot. They were by no means prudish and their language could be most robust with words that would have shocked ordinary Presbyterians and Baptists. They particularly liked the barnyard terms—" and here I'll just stop. He goes on to describe these so vividly that I'd be embarrassed to speak these in front of you, a mixed audience.

I've heard some of the jokes you *gehl-fussicher* (yellow-footed) Schwaben tell, so you don't need to poke fun at my Mennonites. How do I know they are *gehl-fussich?* Because you also told me there was another kind too, which I will not mention here. I heard a story this afternoon which I had learned as a young boy (to illustrate my point). *Warum solen Wir net Lustig sein den Unsere Katz hat Junge. Sie hat aber kein Schuld daran. Der Nachbar's Kadder hat Sie dazu gezwungen.* (Why shouldn't we be jolly, because our cat had kittens. But she didn't have any blame for that at all because the neighbor's tomcat enticed her.)

I grew up thinking the above story was of Mennonite origin, one that all little Mennonite boys learned. But I began wondering, the older I got, whether this wasn't a common, generic German-Russian story—that it wasn't confined to the Mennonites. Just yesterday at this time one of the gentlemen behind the microphone was talking about Adam and Eve and had a little joke about them. I grew up with one and I thought it was strictly of Mennonite origin but now I'm not so sure. Maybe the one I'm going to tell is one that all of you here know and relate to. Even the editorial interpretation of the story may strike a little chord of recognition for some of you. *Der Adam hat sich einmal hingelegt in Paradies und Schlaft. Und dann hat Gott von Ihm ein Frau geschaft. Oh du armer Vater Adam du, deine erste Schlaff war deine letzte Ruh.* (Adam lay down to sleep in Paradise. And then God made from him a wife. Oh you poor Father Adam you, your first sleep was your last rest.)

Again, I don't know if this is strictly Mennonite or whether some of you have heard it before. It is hard to tell, so it makes it more difficult for me to be up here.

The family was the most important ingredient of our ancestors' lives—whether a Mennonite or not. And I think all of you have experienced in your family history something that quite a few of the Mennonites experienced when they lived in the little closed communities in Russia and even in their first ventures in South Dakota, where they too lived in the same little tight communities. In these communities it was not uncommon that first cousins got married; I saw it among other groups around Freeman in addition to the Mennonites—the Kasselers, the Schwaben, the Heilbronners. Now, like in the rest of the world these areas too have become afflicted with divorce. This raised a question in some Mennonite circles that centered on a set of married first cousins that divorced. The question that plagued the community was this: we understand that they are no longer man and wife, but are they still first cousins?

As an aside, US 81 to the Mennonites is a holy highway. A Mennonite's idea of a trip to the Holy Land is to get down to Oklahoma and get on a bus going north on US 81 through many of the little Mennonite towns that lie along this highway in Oklahoma. Then get into Kansas, to McPherson and on to North Newton where there is Bethel College and the Mennonite printing establishment—and, boy, that's almost a Mecca to them. And then keep going north into Nebraska where just a few miles off the highway is Henderson with the second largest Mennonite church in the United States—the largest being at Bern. Then keep right on going into South Dakota to my home town of Freeman, which is the largest Hutterite and Mennonite community in South Dakota. Then there could be a little detour to Mountain Lake, Minnesota, which is the largest Mennonite

community in that state. After getting back to US 81, keep
going north right through Fargo, just a few blocks from where
this meeting is being held and on to Winnipeg, Manitoba, which
has the largest Mennonite population of any city in the world.
This is the Mennonite holy highway.

As all other people, the Mennonites took care of their
young, the infirm, the disabled, and the mentally handicapped.
Speaking of the mentally handicapped, there was a couple that
lived about four miles north of Freeman on highway US 81—we
could still call him a retarded son at the time. They took good
care of him. The son's nickname was Billy Matz. In town
(Freeman) lived the sheriff Jake Huber. Jake was also in the
construction business. (Some of you from the area may
remember Jake Huber.) One morning Jake was going north on
the Mennonite highway to a construction job. A little ways
ahead of him on the road he saw there was something large in
the ditch that he had never seen there before. As he got closer
he saw that right close to where Billy Matz lived someone had
gotten too close to the shoulder of the road with a load of hay
and had caused the hay rack to tip over. He saw too the wheels
of the rack pointed skyward, and on top of it saw a very
disconsolate Billy Matz. So Jake Huber stopped his car, and he
said, ""Billy Matz, *was ist doh basiert?*" And Billy Matz very
glumly said, "*Der heu wagon ist umgesturzt.*" "Yes, I see that,"
said Jake Huber. "*Denkt du net du sollst dein Vater sagen?*"
"*Nei*" replied Billy Matz. "*Vater weists ess, er ist unter dem heu.*"
(Jake Huber asked Billy Matz what happened. The reply was
that the hay rack tipped over. Then Jake Huber asked Billy
Matz if he didn't think he should tell his father. Billy Matz
replied, "Father already knows about it, he is under the hay.")

I think the Mennonite community is old enough now so
that we can begin pointing out differences from other German-
Russian groups. One thing that was greatly different was the
words that we were allowed to use that you in other denominations used in your daily conversations. There were some that
were denied us. The first to come to mind, one that was very

important because it appears in the Bible twice—in Matthew 5:37 and again in James 5:12—was, and I quote: "But above all things my brethren, swear not neither by heaven, neither by the earth, neither by any other oath. Let your yea be yea and your nay be nay, lest you fall into condemnation." As far as the Mennonites are concerned, swearing an oath is not allowed. It is an absolute because of its explicitness, because it is in the Bible twice, and it says let your yea be yea and your nay be nay. So in my daily conversations as a child I was not allowed to use words such as *sicher* (definitely) and *gewiss* (certainly, positively, absolutely) because it exceeded the parameters of yea and nay. Also we were not allowed to swear an oath in court (of course, we weren't supposed to be in court in the first place). We were allowed to affirm, but not swear. So when the tax man (assessor) came around to assess the tax, you could affirm that what you had said was the truth, etc.

Next on the list of forbidden words was the word *Gott,* depending of course entirely on how it was used. "Thou shalt not take the name of the Lord thy God in vain for the Lord will not hold him guiltless that taketh his name in vain." When I was playing outside and if I said "*ach Gott,*" my elders would pounce on me with a vengeance. My grandmother who was my staunchest ally when I got into trouble, too would pounce on me like a plain old common crone and holler at me. That word was not allowed. Yet, however, these older people would use the word *Gott* in a way that mystified me as a child. But I realized later that they used the word *Gott* when they were taking about God. (In other words, the name was not used in vain.)

The following is probably the only story I have that was told by colony Hutterites. One of their ships on which they were coming from Russia had one Hutterite who was absolutely terrified of the ocean. He was petrified and every time the ship rolled a bit and every time a little breeze (wave) ran by he would run to the ship's captain and say, "Oh captain, my captain, are we going to capsize, are we going to drown, are we all going to our death?" The captain soon realized he had a very paranoid Hutterite on his hands, and he told him, "We have not been in danger, but if we get into serious trouble and you come and bother me with your questions you will distract me from my attention and thus add to our danger." He continued, "If you really want to know if we are in trouble, you go down to the bottom of the ship where the men are stoking the furnaces. Those guys are a wild and tough bunch and they have been all around the world and they know the oceans of the world forward and backward. They know when the ocean is smooth and when we're in trouble. But I must caution you they are a lusty (profane) lot, and they swear terribly. But that's alright because once they stop swearing you'll know they are scared. When that happens you can start to say your prayers." Well, it didn't take very long when along comes another little zephyr to rock the boat a little bit. And this paranoid Hutterite found the ladder and headed down into the boiler room where these guys were stoking the fires. All the other Hutterites gathered around the hole into which he had descended, to see (or hear) his reaction. When the paranoid Hutterite came back up, and it didn't take long, he was gray and shaken and scared. But he punched his fists together, cast his eyes heavenward and said, "*Gott sei dank sie fluchen noch.*" (The Lord be praised, they are still swearing.)

If someone used the name of the Lord in vain, and he wasn't a Mennonite, it wasn't so bad. We talked about it. There used to be an evangelist from Mitchell by the name of Crouch (some of you may be old enough to remember him when he came to Freeman to hold revival meetings, renting a hall off of main street). He would put the people down on the sawdust path. At Freeman we didn't have or refer to the term "homeless people," but we had such a guy. He was a derelict. He would pick scraps off the street. He didn't have a regular place to sleep. One bitter cold night he came into this hall where Rev. Crouch was holding the revival meeting. Rev. Crouch was elated to see Bill (the derelict) come in there and he stopped the service and looked

at Bill and said, "Brother, welcome, are you seeking the Lord?"
And Bill said, "Golly, is he lost?"

Now we could tell that story because it wasn't a Mennonite
that was involved and it was in the English language, so that
was O.K. In church we could talk freely about the mishaps that
occurred on our daily pilgrimage to perfection. (That's why I
had to change the title of my talk after I got the letter from
Victor Knell—now I had to concentrate on those pratfalls that
these people took on their imperfect travels on the road to a
perfect life.) So we could laugh about things that went wrong.

One of the favorite subjects was my wife's paternal
grandfather—old grandfather Gering called Hanzul. (I never
knew the gentleman. He died while I was still a youngster.)
Hansoe was a character. He was not very tall, but he was quite
stout. He was a man of firm convictions, and he was very much
a realist. When he went to town to buy some clothes it really
aggravated him that he had to pay as much for articles of
clothing (overalls, etc.) as a fellow who was six feet tall and
weighed over 300 pounds. Such a fellow obviously needed much
more material for his clothes and he had to pay as much as that
fellow did. Why should he pay as much for a size 7½ shoe as
that other fellow did for a size 12? It just didn't make sense.
Consequently he bought the largest size clothes available that
he could wear without losing them. It was his way of retaliat-
ing; he was not going to be victimized. Consequently he was not
a Beau Brummel of the cornfield. He was probably the most
shabbily dressed man in east Freeman.

One Sunday morning he was sitting in church and the
fellow next to him nudged him and pointed down. Here among
the superfluous cloth there was a bunch of unbuttoned
buttons—he had forgotten to button his trousers, and as badly
as the trousers fit he never even noticed it until it was pointed
out to him. He bided his time. At the time our people still knelt
to pray—today we have gotten too sophisticated for that and
no longer kneel to pray. So when the congregation knelt to pray
and everyone else had their hands folded in prayer, his hands

were busy matching buttonholes with buttons. Finally the prayer was over and the Amen said. Everyone got up from their knees to sit down except my wife's grandfather. He remained kneeling like a guy with a *hexaschuss*—he couldn't get up. All at once he gave a mighty lurch and *bing,* a button hit the ceiling. What happened was that his vest had not been buttoned either, and he had buttoned the vest to the trousers. (Stories like these were legitimate game for humor.)

Another time we had foot-washing in our church—I remember it well. It was dropped in the thirties, about the time we switched from the German to the English in our church services. After communion would come the foot-washing. The girls would bring the water up front and the big basins. The fathers then would be first. They would go up front two by two, take off each other's shoes and wash each other's feet as an act of humility, as Christ did to his disciples after the first communion. Well this grandfather of my wife was not quite up to the spirit of things. He was not about to wash feet with just anybody. So he would loiter outside the church until either Grandfather Schwartz or Grandfather Senner came to church. Then he would go in with him so he could wash feet with one of his buddies. This particular Sunday morning, his children told me, Grandpa Schwartz came to church and Grandpa Gering was waiting for him. So they went into church together and soon it was their turn to wash feet. So they went up front. Grandpa Schwartz then proceeded to take off Grandpa Gering shoes, and as friends will, he whispered to him but with such a loud whisper that it was heard all over the little church. The whisper was, "*Ei, ei, das ist aber nötig.*" (My oh my but this is necessary.) Grandma was so embarrassed she didn't go to church for two weeks. She couldn't stand to face the other ladies.

With their music they had quite a bit of fun. But here again I don't know if these are generic tales told by all German-Russians or whether they are just Mennonite tales. Here is one they accused my great-grandfather of, until a couple of years ago when I found a Hutterite minister in a colony to whom I told the story. He said, "Oh, but that happened in the colonies a long time ago before your great-grandfather was around." So here is the story, and it comes from two different places, so I don't know with which religious denomination it originated. The story is, according to the Mennonite source, that my great-grandfather kleiner Andrew Graber was the *vorsinger* (lead singer) in church, which meant that he had the only songbook with the words; they didn't have enough books. So he would get up in front of the congregation and read a line and the congregation would sing the line. Then he would read another line and the people would sing the same line. This one particular Sunday morning at services he got up and announced the hymn "Grosser Gott Wir Loben Dich" (Holy God We Praise Thy Name). So now the tune was fixed in the congregation's mind. He got out the book to look at the words. But, my goodness, he had gotten some of the grease from the cracklings he had on his fingers and in turn on his glasses, which had gotten so greasy he couldn't see the words clearly. After he had announced the song, he took off his glasses and said, "*Was ist los mit meine Brille, sie ist mit fett geschmiert.*" (What is wrong with my glasses? They are smeared with fat.) And the congregation began to sing using the words which he had just spoken. He then said, "*Ach liebe Leute sei doch stille; Ich spreche nur von meine Brille.*" (But dear people be quiet; I'm only talking about my glasses.) And the congregation sang the same words. (I don't know how they finally got it straightened out.)

My Hutterite friend told me of an instance in which a cow owned by a prairie Hutterite (a Hutterite not living in the colony) gave birth to twins. At the time it was a more unusual event than it is today. He and his family were so overjoyed that they decided that one of the calves was the Lord's calf and the profit made from raising the calf would go the Lord. Lo and behold, one of the calves died. Guess whose calf it was! On Sunday they went to church, and in this case the congregation was in the process of getting some English language hymn

books. The choir sang some of the songs from the hymnal that
the congregation would be learning. Imagine the congregation's
surprise when the choir began singing "The Half Has Not Been
Told." As the choir was singing this hymn, the prairie Hutterite
was listening, but he didn't know English very well. He said to
himself, "My goodness, they're singing the calf has been sold."
He got very disturbed as well as his family. Additionally the
choir sang all the stanzas. He felt that the eyes of the congregation and choir were on him and his family. After they got home,
he and the family were unanimous that indeed it was their calf,
not the Lord's, that had died.

    Church discipline was very strict. Based on Matthew
18:15-17, "If your brother sins against you, go and tell him his
fault between thee and him alone; if he shall hear thee, thou
hast gained thy brother. But if he will not hear thee, then take
with thee one or two more, that in the mouth of two or three
witnesses every word may be established. And if he shall
neglect (refuse) to hear them, tell it to the church; but if he
neglect to hear the church, let him be unto thee as an heathen
man and a publican." I have four short stories for illustration.

    The first deals with disputing parties that had to have
witnesses at a meeting to settle their differences. This one man
who was the chief witness took with him another man when the
two contestants got together. The first contestant presented his
side very well, to which the chief witness said, "*Bruder du
hasch recht.*" (Brother you are right.) Then he turned to the
second contestant who was equally convincing, and the chief
witness said to him, "*Aber Bruder du hasch auch recht.*" (But
brother you are right too.) The second witness present grabbed
the chief witness by the arm, shook him and said, "*Aber Bruder,
die können beide nicht recht sein.*" (But, brother, both of them
cannot be right.) The chief witness turned to the other witness
and said, "*Bruder, du hasch aber auch recht.*" (Brother, you are
right too.)

    My grandfather got caught playing pool one time, so he
had to apologize to the church or take the consequences of being

expelled from the congregation. My grandfather was in a predicament—how do you translate "shooting pool" into German. You see, shooting pool was a Yankee indiscretion and it had been told the preacher that my grandfather was shooting pool and my grandfather admitted it. So on Sunday morning after the services the preacher called a congregational meeting for the purpose of discussing discipline. In relating the purpose of the meeting the preacher said, "*Ess ist uns gesagt worden das der Seb Schrag tut bull schiessa.*" (It has been said that he was shooting the bull.)

There was a lady who had three sons, and one of the sons built a home for her across the road from where he lived so that he could look after her in her old age. This one Sunday afternoon she looked out of her window, and what does she see but a group of Mennonite boys carrying guns—on a Sunday afternoon—they were hunting. What was she to do? Well, there was only one thing she could do and that was to tell the church fathers about it so they could take some disciplinary action. (I must inject here that Parker, South Dakota, was the county seat of Turner County, and there was a lot of anti-German feeling there during World War I. Parker was a place of ill repute as far as the Mennonites were concerned. But they had to go there for some of their business dealings because of the courthouse.) Anyhow, here came these gun-carrying Mennonite boys on Sunday, and this lady felt that she had to report them to the church authorities so proper disciplinary action could be taken. But she wasn't sure who the boys were. So she stepped out on the front porch, her arms rolled up in her apron, and she said, "*Yoo hoo, buba, wer senn Ihr dann?*" (Yoo Hoo, boys who are you?) Little Charlie, who was closest to the house, and who was sharp and knew what she had in mind, said, "*Mir senn Englische von Parker.*" (We are English people from Parker.) And she said, "*Ach Gott sei dank, gehen eich.*" (Oh God be praised, get along.)

There are several things to be taken into consideration in this my last and favorite story.

When I was a young lad I'd hear my dad and my uncle
Julius, when working together, hear one of them saying
"Zensele witt boom boom," with both of them breaking out in a
grin. When I asked what this was all about, they would say it
was something that happened so long ago that they'd forgotten
it, and they refused to tell. It came the time I married my wife
that we went to Kansas to visit distant relatives and relatives
on both sides to introduce each other to them. One person we
visited was my wife's grandmother's brother John P. O. Graber.
(He once owned a furniture store in Hutchinson.) John Graber
said, "So you're from South Dakota (I said yes.) the home of
Zensele witt boom boom." I said, "Do you know that?" His reply
was, "Why sure, doesn't everybody?" So I said to him, "Would
you sing it for me so I can write it down?" And he was honored
and flattered that I would ask him. So he gave me the words to
the poem.

When we got back to South Dakota and the opportunity
presented itself when Uncle Julius and Dad were together, I
said, "Have you guys ever heard this?" as I proceeded to sing
the first verse. They were astounded and asked where I got
that. I said, "Well my wife's grandmother's brother John P. O.
Graber told me, and I think it is really remarkable that a man
old enough to be your father remembers every word of it while
you guys told me long ago that you couldn't remember it." After
I read all the verses John Graber had given me, they said, "He
isn't so sharp; he left out a verse." So they sang it for me and
I wrote it down.

John P. O. Graber could tell this story about *Zensele witt
boom boom* because he was a Presbyterian. He had been kicked
out of the Mennonite Church because he played a trumpet solo,
so he was no longer bound by the rules of the Mennonite
Church. What happened was that my ancestors were of Amish
background but made the change and became members of the
General Conference of Mennonites (the most liberal of the
Mennonites) when they came from Russia in 1874. In becoming
part of the General Mennonite Conferences they kicked over

the traces and started a Swiss Choral Society, started getting musical instruments in church, and started a Literary Society to give budding young artists a chance to show their skills.

There were two people central to this *Zensele witt boom boom* story. One was Joachim Miller, whose nickname, which he despised, was Zensele. The other was John M. Schrag, whose nickname was Schimmel; John was quite a poet.

It had its start when Zensele was about to get married; he had to go to Silver Lake, about four to five miles north of Freeman on the Mennonite Highway, to get a load of sand to mortar some rocks together for a chimney and some for the foundation for his bride's home. As he was going for the sand, he drove by the farm of a prairie Hutterite, David Hofer. As he was passing the farm the dogs came out and harassed the team to the point that Zensele was afraid he would lose the harness and the wagon. He had to pass the farm again on the return trip with the loaded wagon, and it was even more of a disaster. He dreaded having to come back the next day for another load. So he borrowed a muzzle-loading shotgun that he said he loaded with corn—some people thought it was with rocks. At any rate the next day when he came to the Hofer farm and the dogs came out, he shot and injured one. And, Oh, terrible things happened. It was at this point in time that Johann Schrag had to write a poem for the Literary Society. For this he picked this whole episode as a topic, and he skillfully wrote it to the meter that could be sung to the tune of "Ich Bin der Doktor Eisenbart." After he sang it, it caught on. Zensele was so embarrassed he went to the church fathers and complained. They had Schimmel Johann apologize to Zensele in public, which he did. But the people of the congregation had to promise nevermore to sing the song, so my dad and uncle Julius were honor bound not to let it out. So I would never had heard it in its entirety if John P. O. Graber had not tooted his horn and been kicked out of church, leaving him free to tell me.

Here are the words:

Wie es an allen ist bekant	*As is known to everyone*
Zensele witt boom boom	*Refrain*
Der Zensele fuhr einmal nach sand	*Zensel went (drove) after some sand*
Zensele witt boom boom	*Refrain*
Er nam mit sich auch eine flint	*He took along a shotgun*
Zensele, Zensele witt boom boom	*Refrain*
Zum hunden schiesen wo er findt	*To shoot dogs where he found them.*
Zensele witt boom boom	*Refrain*
Beim David war das erste haus	*The first house was at David's*
Zensele witt boom boom	*Refrain*
Da wirklich kamen hunden raus	*Truly, dogs came from the yard*
Zensele witt boom boom	*Refrain*
Der Knab hat sich nicht lang bedacht	*The young man did not pause long to decide*
Zensele, Zensele witt boom boom	
Auf einmal hat es los gekracht	*Refrain*
Zensele witt boom boom	*Suddenly he fired the shotgun.*
	Refrain
Dass kann man garnicht angenahm	*One can't at all accept the claim*
Zensele witt boom boom	*Refrain*
Das es mit korn geladen hat	*That the shotgun was loaded with corn*
Zensele witt boom boom	
Ein kugel muss gewesen sein	*Refrain*
Zensele, Zensele witt boom boom	*It must have been a bullet instead*
Von hinten flog es bis zum aug	*Refrain*
Zensele witt boom boom	*(Because) it penetrated from the rear to the eye.*
	Refrain
So sehte der David das gefuhr	*David observed what had occurred*
Zensele witt boom boom	*Refrain*
Da macht er sich gleich auf die spuhr	*So he immediately got on the rail*
Zensele witt boom boom	*Refrain*
Zum laufen war er doch zu faul	*To walk he was too lazy*
Zensele, Zensele witt boom boom	*Refrain*

Und setzte sich auf seinses Gaul   *So he sat himself upon a horse.*

Zensele witt boom boom   *Refrain*

Nun als er zu dem wagen kamm   *So when he (David) came to the wagon*

Zensele witt boom boom   *Refrain*

Er reiszt die flint von Knabe ab   *He tore the shotgun from the young*

Zensele witt boom boom   *man's hand.*

Und schlug sie auf das wagen rad   *Refrain*

Zensele, Zensele witt boom boom   *And smashed it on the wagon wheel*

Auf tausend stücke quer und grad   *Refrain*

Zensele witt boom boom   *Into a thousand pieces angled and*

straight.

Refrain

Dan war der Knab doch sehr besorgt   *Thus this took care of the young man*

Zensele witt boom boom   *Refrain*

Denn er hat die flinte nur geborgt   *For he had only borrowed the shotgun*

Zensele witt boom boom   *Refrain*

Da versetzte er sein huld and thun   *It put a mortgage on everything he*

Zensele, Zensele witt boom boom   *owned*

Und das reicht Ihm nicht lang dazu   *Refrain*

Zensele witt boom boom   *And this didn't take long to do.*

Refrain

Acknowledgments

The publishers gratefully acknowledge the following for permission to reprint articles by Reuben Goertz.

"Wedding Bells Ringing, Skeletons in Closets Jingling," *Work Paper* of the American Historical Society of Germans from Russia, No. 17 (April 1975):3-7.

"German Russian Homes: Here and There, Now and Then," *Clues* (Lincoln, NE: American Historical Society of Germans from Russia, 1976):31-50.

"An Irreverant Mennonite Casts Sidelong Glances at His Volga Compatriots," *Journal of the American Historical Society of Germans from Russia* 1.3 (Winter 1978):23-27.

"Pioneering in Dakota Territory," *Journal of the American Historical Society of Germans from Russia* 5.3 (Fall 1982):5-11.

"Pioneers in Petticoats," *Papers of the Fifteenth Dakota History Conference,* edited by H. W. Blakely (Madison, SD: Dakota State College, 1984):509-520.

"Reinhold Dewald and Relief Cattle for Germany," *Journal of the American Historical Society of Germans from Russia* 11.1 (Spring 1988):ii-9.

"Folktales—Facts or Fiction?" *Papers of the Twenty-second Annual Dakota History Conference,* compiled by Arthur R. Huseboe (Sioux Falls, SD: Center for Western Studies, 1990):266-279.

"From Missionary to Mummy: A South Dakotan Comes Home," *Papers of the Twenty-Fourth Annual Dakota History Conference,* compiled by Arthur R. Huseboe (Sioux Falls, SD: Center for Western Studies, 1992):170-179.

"My Sullied Saints: Things I Did Not Learn in Catechism," *Heritage Review* 24.1 (1994):3-8.

Index of Names of Persons